Milarepa's Kungfu

Milarepa's Kungfu

MAHĀMUDRĀ IN HIS SONGS OF REALIZATION

Karl Brunnhölzl

Foreword by Dzogchen Ponlop Rinpoche

Wisdom

Wisdom Publications
199 Elm Street
Somerville, MA 02144 USA
wisdomexperience.org

Library of Congress Cataloging-in-Publication Data
Names: Brunnhölzl, Karl, author.
Title: Milarepa's Kungfu: Mahāmudrā in his songs of realization / Karl Brunnhölzl.
Description: First. | Somerville: Wisdom Publications, 2021. |
    Includes bibliographical references.
Identifiers: LCCN 2021012144 (print) | LCCN 2021012145 (ebook) |
    ISBN 9781614296614 (hardcover) | ISBN 9781614296621 (ebook)
Subjects: LCSH: Mi-la-ras-pa, 1040–1123—Teachings. | Meditation—Buddhism. |
    Mahāmudrā (Tantric rite) | Spiritual life—Buddhism.
Classification: LCC BQ7950.M557 B78 2021 (print) | LCC BQ7950.M557 (ebook) |
    DDC 294.3/923092—dc23
LC record available at https://lccn.loc.gov/2021012144
LC ebook record available at https://lccn.loc.gov/2021012145

ISBN 978-1-61429-661-4   ebook ISBN 978-1-61429-662-1
25 24 23 22 21   5 4 3 2 1

Cover art by R.D. Salga, reprinted with permission from Dzogchen Ponlop Rinpoche.
Cover and interior design by Gopa & Ted2, Inc. Set in Athelas 10.65/15.

Printed on acid-free paper that meets the guidelines for permanence and durability of
the Production Guidelines for Book Longevity of the Council on Library Resources.

Printed in the United States of America.

Contents

Mind-Bending Song
Foreword by Dzogchen Ponlop Rinpoche

HAVE YOU EVER stood at a vista point that looked out over a vast landscape to the meeting point of endless ocean and brilliant sky? It's a joyful, speechless, and breathtaking experience. We are carried right to that awe-inspiring point as we read Milarepa's songs, but with one difference. Milarepa was sitting at the vista point of reality and looking straight at its true nature, an expansive, profound, and blissful view.

If, in the course of things, you find yourself there in Mila's same spot looking straight at that view, see how your mind begins to bend! It bends to the point that you won't even recognize it as mind. At that moment, you glimpse the nature of your present mind, the same nature Milarepa saw—open, spacious, blissful, and free from thoughts. To say the least, mind is not at all rigid; in fact, it is infinitely supple and flexible. This awesome mind is quite funny, too. If you confine it, it wants to escape. If you let it go, it just stays. If you look at it, there is nothing there. When you are not looking, it's full of spontaneous creative energy and continuously manifesting in a multitude of ways, as wisdom, love, and drama as well.

Like many yogins of India, Milarepa often expressed his experiences in spontaneous songs, as a way to recollect or communicate them to others. These songs are classically known as *dohas* (couplets). Most famous poetry draws its inspiration from deep emotional experiences. But for Milarepa, his inspiration was his realization of mind and its reality.

"Seeing is believing" is a phrase we often hear. It makes sense and it's mostly how we operate. When I hear it, I'm reminded of this view—the reality we can't believe until we see it. Seeing is a direct experience that goes beyond thought's imaginations. As Milarepa developed certainty in what he saw, the view of the nature of mind, he gained confidence in that view. That is believing, or unshakable conviction.

That breathtaking view from the vista point can become part of your everyday experience if you sit there frequently. Otherwise it may simply remain as a picture in your device. Not only may you not be able to find that picture when you need it, you may not even remember that experience! So, seeing reality alone is not enough to gain complete freedom from mundane thoughts and confusion. The view may be intriguing but still it's just a momentary experience, which will soon pass. In order for that experience become more consistent or continuous, you need to familiarize yourself with it again and again. Deepening the view through familiarization is what's called "meditation."

When you are able to be at that viewpoint with certainty at all times, then all you do is embraced by the aura of that vast view and meditation. This is what's known as "action" or "conduct." It enables you to act with love and awareness and to see things more clearly within the experience of openness and spaciousness. This brings great joy in life because now you are seeing the reality in everything your mind touches.

Finally, as you go deeper, there's a sense of oneness of the seer, the view, and the experience. There's no gap between you and the reality. This is the result of view, meditation, and action becoming one with your whole being. This is called "fruition," the revelation of your full potential, and being able to manifest that will free your mind from delusion and pain. You can find peace and freedom in every moment of life; thus, life becomes beautiful and joyful.

In this book, Dr. Karl Brunnhölzl, our Nalandabodhi Mitra, unveils the secret of view, meditation, and action as sung by the king of yogins, Milarepa. This book is certain to open a new dimension for your mind and bring the mind-bending experience of the yogi into your heart on the spot! These teachings of Milarepa are a timely and straight-to-the-heart wisdom that will surely benefit many in this century and beyond.

I truly appreciate Mitra Karl accepting my request to teach this doha in the beginning, turning that into a book in the middle, and bringing it into our world at the end. With heartfelt gratitude, I close with the aspiration that all who even glance at this book may see the reality and free their mind.

Dzogchen Ponlop Rinpoche
Nalanda West
Seattle, WA

Preface

ALLOW ME a few words on the origin and title of this book. Some years ago, Dzogchen Ponlop Rinpoche, the spiritual director of Nalandabodhi, received a phone call from his guru, Khenpo Tsultrim Gyamtso Rinpoche, during which Khenpo Rinpoche told him that it would be very important for him, Dzogchen Ponlop Rinpoche, to teach his students the Milarepa song called *Ultimate View, Meditation, Conduct, and Fruition.* However, with the rationale that he, Dzogchen Ponlop Rinpoche, was "out of town" (referring to Seattle), he called me instead (you see how these things go) and said, "You do it." Since I did not want to ignore his request and did not find anyone else to pass this on to, I gave a series of talks on Milarepa's song, using Khenpo Rinpoche's own brief comments on it, as well as other Milarepa songs that discuss the same themes. Subsequently, these talks were offered as an internal Nalandabodhi publication; now, in a thoroughly revised and slightly expanded version, they are published as this little booklet.

As for the title, in its original meaning in China, *kungfu* (more correctly spelled *gōngfu*) generally indicates any kind of discipline or skill that is achieved through hard work, patience, practice, and the necessary time to complete it—not only and not necessarily martial arts. *Gōng* (功) means "skillful work," "hard training," or "endeavor," and *fu* (夫) means "time spent." In our context here, the term refers to Milarepa's diligent and skillful training in the techniques to realize the nature of his mind and benefit countless sentient beings.

Milarepa's perseverance is illustrated by the famous story of how he said farewell to his principal student, Gampopa. The two had already said their goodbyes, and Gampopa was walking down the mountain, when Milarepa called him back up and said, "I have one last parting instruction to give to you, which is the most profound of everything I taught you," and he pulled up his cotton robe to expose his naked behind. Gampopa saw that it was covered with calluses from Milarepa's many decades of sitting diligently in meditation posture on the hard rocks of different mountain caves.

I'd like to thank Khenpo Tsultrim Gyamtso Rinpoche as the master singer and commentator of many songs of awakening by the great yogī Milarepa and other mahāsiddhas, as well as his own songs of realization, and for being the original inspiration behind this booklet. Heartfelt thanks also go to Dzogchen Ponlop Rinpoche for giving me the opportunity to dive deeper into Milarepa's wisdom mind through giving talks on his song and editing them into a book. On the practical side of things, my gratitude and appreciation go to Daniel Aitken at Wisdom Publications for his willingness to make this publication available to a wider audience, as well as to Laura Cunningham, my skilled and friendly editor at Wisdom.

Introduction

....

Milarepa: From Mass Murderer to Buddha

Milarepa, commonly considered to be Tibet's most famous yogī, turned his career around from having murdered many of his relatives through black magic into becoming a buddha in only twelve years: quite an accomplishment! Thereafter, he spent the rest of his life helping other people to also become buddhas. At one point, one of his students said to him, "You must be an emanation or an incarnation of a great buddha or bodhisattva, because you managed to purify all your negative karma and become a fully awakened buddha in only twelve years." Milarepa became upset about this remark and answered, "Saying something like that means you have no trust in the power and efficiency of the buddha's teachings to actually work for everybody. I am neither a bodhisattva nor an incarnation or emanation of anybody. I started out as a completely ordinary being, as you can see from my early life, when I murdered many people. The only thing I claim for myself as a positive feature is that I really saw that the buddha's teaching is the only thing that could help me to purify what I did and that I then had enough perseverance to actually do what was necessary for that."

It is well known that after Milarepa had met his guru, Marpa Lotsāwa, Marpa put Milarepa through years of mind-boggling physical and mental difficulties. Finally, Milarepa received the instructions he desired from Marpa and then left to put them into practice. After that, he never saw his teacher again. Not only had he received all the instructions necessary for the entire path to buddhahood, but more amazingly, he remembered and correctly practiced them all.

The Setting of This Song

Milarepa always sang his songs by specifically tailoring them to his diverse audiences, which came from all walks of life. He not only sang for his advanced yogic disciples (both male and female) but also to his sister Peta, village people, farmers, hunters, shepherds, robbers, scholars, kings, ghosts, demons, mundane and supramundane deities, dharma protectors, and even animals. Thus, the themes of his songs are as variegated as the different backgrounds, needs, emotional hang-ups, and spiritual accomplishments of his audiences. However, in each case, his songs contain a clear message for the addressees in order to benefit them in either a temporary or ultimate manner.

One theme that pervades many of Milarepa's songs is a recounting of his own profound realization, attained primarily through the practice of inner heat (Skt. *caṇḍālī*) and mahāmudrā. *Mahāmudrā* refers to both the ultimate essence of all beings' minds (also known as "buddha nature") and the specific meditation practices that allow for recognizing, becoming familiar with, and fully realizing this essence. The practice of mahāmudrā is not one to be undertaken by beginners on the Buddhist path but one of the most advanced forms of meditation. Thus, those who aspire to engage in mahāmudrā must usually go through a number of preliminary studies and practices in order to gradually familiarize themselves with the ultimate view. Milarepa usually does not discuss these preliminaries in his songs but typically goes right to the very heart of the matter.

His song called *Ultimate View, Meditation, Conduct, and Fruition* was written with a template that is common to a lot of his songs and is also found in other Buddhist teachings. This consists of *view* as the basis or ground, *meditation* as the training in or the familiarization with that view, *conduct* as the natural outflow of having familiarized oneself with the view in meditation, and *fruition* as the final outcome of having fully assimilated and realized the view. As we will see, Milarepa says that the fruition is really nothing different from the view. In this way, we end up with what we started out with.

Ultimate View, Meditation, Conduct, and Fruition is Milarepa's culminating instruction to Rechungpa, his main disciple besides Gampopa. It comes at the end of the thirty-ninth chapter of Milarepa's life story, which is called "The Song of the Wild Asses."

Rechungpa was known to have quite a temper and also possessed some pride due to having obtained many special and precious instructions from the Indian mahāsiddha Tipupa (a student of Nāropa and Maitrīpa) and others, including those of "the dharma cycles of the bodyless ḍākinīs," which Milarepa had not received from Marpa.

One day, Milarepa sent Rechungpa to fetch some water, while he built a fire. Rechungpa got the water but then became engrossed in watching the miraculous display of a wild ass giving birth to a foal on a vast plain. Each of them then gave birth to another foal, with this process continuing progressively until there were one hundred wild asses and one hundred foals frolicking on that plain. Finally, one of the wild asses turned into a wolf and chased all the other asses over a pass. Unknown to Rechungpa, this entire display had been created by Milarepa. Meanwhile, Milarepa had burned all of Rechungpa's scriptures, which he had brought from India under great hardship, except for a few special scrolls. When Rechungpa came back and saw that Milarepa had reduced his precious texts to ashes, he was appalled and in great agony about the loss. Milarepa just said, "You were gone for so long fetching water that I thought you had died. Since I have no use for those texts of yours and they would only distract me from virtuous activity, I burned them. What took you so long?" Angry and dejected, Rechungpa completely lost faith in his guru and announced that he was thinking about going back to Tipupa or some other place. Milarepa answered, "No need to lose faith, son! This is the result that you brought upon yourself through your own distraction, watching all those asses. But if you like shows, I'll give you some shows to watch!"

Milarepa then produced a series of miraculous displays, appearing as Cakrasaṃvara, Hevajra, and other Vajrayāna deities, moving through rocks, sitting on water, letting fire blaze and water gush from his body, and flying through space. Each time, Rechungpa remained unimpressed and petulant, insisting that the only thing that would impress him would be if Milarepa were to give him back his burned texts.

When Milarepa finally flew up in the sky until he was out of sight, deep regret arose in Rechungpa and he regained his faith, realizing that his texts were of no use to him without his guru. Thinking that Milarepa had abandoned him, he became utterly disheartened and jumped off a cliff to kill himself. As he was lying there with his shattered body, the shadow of Milarepa, who was still flying, fell upon him. Rechungpa got up and tried to stumble after Milarepa's shadow, because he was unable to fly with his broken body. Finally, Milarepa manifested himself as three of his own bodies, singing to Rechungpa to encourage him to regret and confess his misbehavior. Rechungpa sang a song in reply and then fervently hugged the central one of Milarepa's three bodies.

Milarepa said, "Rechungpa, if you wish to attain buddhahood, you must be able to meditate in sync with the guru's naked pith instructions. Among your texts, I only preserved the 'dharma cycles of the bodyless ḍākinīs,' because they are of value to me. I burned the others, because there is a danger that you could be led astray by them into the lower, painful realms of saṃsāra." Finally, Milarepa sang his song *Ultimate View, Meditation, Conduct, and Fruition* to Rechungpa, which he said contained the pith instructions that Rechungpa still needed.[1]

1: The Synopsis of View, Meditation, Conduct, and Fruition

MILAREPA'S SONG opens with the following four lines:

> The view is the wisdom of being empty
> Meditation is luminosity without fixation
> Conduct is a continual flow free of attachment
> Fruition is nakedness bare of any stain[2]

This verse is the "sneak preview" or "trailer" for the remaining parts of the song, which discuss each of these topics in more detail. The synopsis here succinctly highlights the essential points of view, meditation, conduct, and fruition, while the following four verses offer comments on each of these. In a sense, the view is the most important element here, being the ground within which the proper meditation, conduct, and fruition of mahāmudrā can arise. In the Mahāmudrā tradition, without the genuine view, or outlook, to begin with, there is really nothing to meditate on, no proper conduct as the enhancement of meditation and realization, and no fruition as the unobscured radiance of mind's luminous spaciousness. Therefore, the view needs to be discussed in the greatest detail.

VIEW—THE OUTLOOK OF OPEN AND SPACIOUS LUMINOSITY

The first line says, "**The view is the wisdom of being empty**." According to Khenpo Tsultrim Gyamtso Rinpoche, we can understand this in many ways, but the main point that Milarepa makes here is that wisdom is empty of everything that obscures it. Primordially existing wisdom, which is another term for the nature of our mind, is empty of all obscurations. From wisdom's own point of view, this wisdom is always completely unobscured and unstained. Unfortunately, this is not the case from our point of view. As its title says, Milarepa's song speaks about view, meditation, conduct, and fruition from the ultimate point of view of how things really are and not so much from how things might appear to those who have not realized ultimate reality.

What Milarepa means when he says "view" here refers to a profound inner experience of our innate nondual and nonconceptual awareness, which is rather different from what we usually understand by "the view" in Buddhism. When Buddhist philosophical schools, such as Madhyamaka, talk about "the view," or we could say "the theory," it usually refers to something written down, something about which somebody is talking, or something that we discuss, read about, or hear about, and then reflect and meditate on. In other words, this kind of "view" has a lot to do with words, concepts, and the understanding that is based on them. In general, when it is said in Buddhism that we need to have the right view, it means to eliminate everything that is supposedly a wrong view and then to ascertain what is supposedly the right view.

Though such an approach may serve as a preliminary for mahāmudrā, what Milarepa talks about here is the direct and blissful experience of nonconceptual wisdom, or the nature of the mind, without any shrouds of dualistic perceptions, thoughts, emotions, or even any Buddhist notions. It is this experience beyond our speech, thoughts, and sense perceptions that is called "the view" here. Students at the beginning of the path of mahāmudrā need to be introduced to this experience of their own mind's nature through a qualified teacher. Once the students experience at least a glimpse of this nature, this represents the actual start of that path on the inside.

In Tibetan and Sanskrit, the words for "view" can also mean something like "outlook," which is more what is meant here. Often in the Buddhist tradition, a difference is made between a view and an outlook. A "view" is more like a philosophical or conceptual framework in which we deal with reasonings and scriptures in order to "get it right," but when we talk about an "outlook," it is a way of seeing or experiencing things that comes from within. It is an experiential quality that informs and pervades not only our meditation but also everything that we do, say, and perceive. This is nothing other than what is usually transmitted through the so-called pointing-out instructions, when the nature of the mind is pointed out or introduced by a qualified teacher to a qualified student through a great variety of skillful means. Obviously, the nature of the mind is not something we can plop in front of us on a table and then say, "Look, this is it." It is a little bit subtler and trickier. There might be a lot of pointing-out efforts on the teacher's side and a lot of efforts by the student to get it, yet there still might not be an actual direct experience of it; it might just be a conceptual understanding.

What Milarepa talks about here when he says "the view" is not the conceptual understanding of some theory, concept, or philosophical system, but the direct experience of the nature of our mind, however brief or tiny a glimpse it may be. The idea here is that if we do not have some basic experience of the nature of the mind, we cannot familiarize ourselves with it, because we do not know what we are supposed to become familiar with. Instead, we just meditate on some kind of a merely conceptual understanding of it.

MEDITATION—SUSTAINING THE VIEW

"**Meditation**," or rather familiarization, is said here to be "**luminosity without fixation**." In mahāmudrā, meditation is nothing other than familiarizing with the view that was introduced and seen: the raw and naked experience of our mind's very own face without any makeup, which initially might just be a glimpse or a brief peek. Therefore, we need to familiarize ourselves more with it and get used to it. Obviously, "luminosity" does not mean something like light in a light bulb; it refers to mind's vivid wakefulness and awareness, as well as its innate purity of any obscurations. The Tibetan word *gom,* which is usually translated as "meditation," actually means "familiarization" or "cultivation."[3] Thus, "meditation" here refers to becoming familiar with the view, which means becoming more and more accustomed to the basic experience of mind's nature.

It is a little bit like eating Tibetan food for the first time. It is a direct experience, but for most people it might be brief and unfamiliar. If we want to get used to Tibetan food, such as butter tea or Tibetan noodle soup, we have to become familiar with it by eating it again and becoming used to its particular taste. Similarly, mahāmudrā meditation means to allow our mind to reconnect with its initial experience of its own nature. This does not mean to try to fabricate, repeat, imitate, or conjure up this experience in any way, but to allow for reencountering it in a meditation that is free from any expectations for certain desired experiences to arise and free from any fears of certain undesired experiences arising.

From that point of view there is not really anything to meditate on as a kind of conceptual object, or for that matter, any object at all. As the famous *Supplication to the Tagpo Kagyü* says:

> Just as it is taught that nondistraction is the actual meditation,
> this meditator rests in nothing but this uncontrived state,
> the fresh nature of whatever thought that may arise—
> bless me to be free of a mind with something to meditate on!

When we meditate *on* something, there is already some dualism involved: there is a meditator and an object to focus on. In many meditations this is part of the process and thus unavoidable, but what Milarepa and the *Supplication* talk about here is letting mind's own luminosity, mind's basic nature, which is lucid, clear, vivid, aware, and awake, rest in its own natural and uncontrived state. This is also completely free of any fixation, which includes there not being any meditator or anything to meditate on, there being no object, no subject, and no duality whatsoever. Nor is there any hope or expectation or fear. There is no hope that we reencounter our initial basic experience of the nature of the mind (which is the view), nor is there any fear that we will not encounter it again.

CONDUCT—MEDITATION IN ACTION

Milarepa continues, "**Conduct is a continual flow free of attachment.**" It is not by accident that this sounds similar to meditation, because conduct is basically just the continuation of the meditative process outside of meditation. Meditation is what we do in our formal meditation sessions, and conduct is what we do in the same way when we are not in formal meditation but engaged in "meditation in action" in all our daily activities. The experiences and realizations that are cultivated in mahāmudrā meditation cannot be reserved for the times when we sit on our meditation cushion; they need to be integrated into every aspect of our daily lives. In mahāmudrā, "conduct" just means to reconnect with and rest within the nature of the mind as much as possible while acting from within that state. If we are able to do that, it is said that whatever we do is fine, even if it appears to be strange and weird to other people.

There are many stories about Indian, Tibetan, Chinese, Japanese, and other Buddhist masters who acted like crazy people from an ordinary point of view and were not really understood by anybody. Those people are said to have realized something that other people did not, and their actions flowed forth from the perspective of constantly experiencing mind's nature, not from an ordinary perspective of what is good and bad or what we are supposed to do or not to do. Therefore, conduct here is not about any rules, any dos or don'ts, or any vows that we take and then have to keep. The only vow that we take here is to try to reconnect with or rest within the basic nature of the mind as much as we can—and act from that state and not from our usual states of attachment, aggression, ignorance, pride, envy, and so on.

However, as Milarepa warns below in his song, if we try to engage in crazy or outrageous behavior without the necessary underlying realization and compassion, there is not only no benefit to such behavior but it will encourage wrong views and cause harm to both ourselves and others.

Fruition—Buddha Nature Undressed

Finally, Milarepa says, "**Fruition is nakedness bare of any stain.**" "Fruition" refers to the state of not falling back into not resting or being within the nature of the mind, but solely remaining within, living within, and being that nature continuously. At that point, there is no difference between meditating and not meditating, or doing anything else. When we look back at the view, Milarepa says that it is "**the wisdom of being empty.**" According to Khenpo Rinpoche, from its own perspective, this wisdom always has been, is, and will be empty of stains. The difference between the view (or the ground) and the fruition is merely that, finally, from the perspective of what is actually experienced (or from the perspective of the one who has traveled the Buddhist path), the stains of the ground—of buddha nature—are gone. Ultimately speaking, the stains were already gone, or rather never existed, in the first place, since the nature of our mind is actually never obscured by anything. However, as ordinary beings, we do not realize this. Once it is finally realized that mind's nature has always been free from all afflictions, obscurations, and trouble, and is endowed with infinite intrinsic buddha qualities (such as nondual wisdom, all-encompassing and inexhaustible compassion, and the power to help others in many skillful ways), that is called "fruition." The situation of sentient beings is like sitting on top of a huge golden nugget in the earth without knowing it. Once they unearth it, they realize that this pure gold was not only never affected by the dirt around it but is available as a powerful means to fulfill all their wishes.

"Nakedness" here refers to experiencing the nature of our mind, just as it is, without our usual hodgepodge of dressing it up in concepts, thoughts, mental afflictions, dualistic perceptions, values, and judgments. It is often said that our buddha nature (which is also called "luminosity," "wisdom," "ordinary mind," "mind as such," and "great bliss" in Mahāmudrā) is dressed up in many layers of afflictions, such as ignorance, anger, attachment, pride, and jealousy. When these "garments" or "costumes" are stripped away, the basic awareness that is mind's nature is "naked" or uncovered, without even a fig leaf of embarrassment, free from all unawareness, duality, and emotional upheaval. It shows itself in its completely natural, uncontrived state, without any additives, preservatives, or artificial colors.

2. The View Is Not a Theory but an Experience

AFTER THE FIRST verse of the song has given us the preview of the ultimate view, meditation, conduct, and fruition, Milarepa continues with more details about the view of Mahāmudrā (after the preview follows the view, so to speak):

> With the view, which is this wisdom of being empty,
> there is the danger of it getting lost in mere platitudes
> If certainty about the heart of the matter does not arise,
> the clinging to a self will not become free through words
> Therefore, the keenest certainty is absolutely essential

Khenpo Rinpoche explains that when we talk about wisdom being empty of stains or wisdom being empty of everything that it is not, it is not like a glass being empty of water or a cow being empty of being a horse. It is more like forms in a dream clearly appearing but being empty of any solid or real existence. In the same way, nonconceptual wisdom is also said to be dream-like in the sense that it appears or is experienced clearly and vividly but cannot be solidified as being a truly existent "this" or "that." We cannot grasp, pinpoint, or nail it down in any way. The experience of the nature of the mind is something elusive; the more we try to get a hold of it, the less that works. The experience is more like a gift; we cannot catch it, force it, or squeeze it forth from our mind.

In the animated movie *Kung Fu Panda*, the master, who is an old turtle, speaks about the past, future, and present, saying:

> The past is history, the future is a mystery, but today is a gift—
> that's why they call it "the present."

Likewise, any experience of the nature of the mind can only happen right now in the present moment, not in what is already past nor in what may happen in the future. If awareness can stay within the experience of the present moment of our mind's nature, that's it. But this is not something that we can produce, acquire, or repeat. Therefore, it is a gift in each moment, not something that can be "obtained" or "attained." In other words, our dualistic mind needs to relax, let go, and step back, clearing the stage for mind's true nature to make its appearance. It's like our mind's nature saying to us, "Don't call us; we'll call you."

Thus, in Mahāmudrā, "I" as a person cannot even really realize mind's nature; it's more a question of "me" getting out of the way and simply letting the wisdom mind be what it is and do what it does, without my ego or dualistic mind interfering with it. When we say, "I want to realize wisdom" or "I want to become a buddha," from a buddha's point of view that is a contradiction in terms and we are not making sense, because in being a buddha or realizing mind's nature, there is no "I" or "me" in the first place. Nor is there anything to realize that is not already present right within our mind. The nature of the mind is said to be what we ultimately are, whereas everything that has to do with "I" and "mine" is what obscures this nature. Thus, it is difficult to realize.

In her *Vajra Lines of Self-Arising Mahāmudrā*, the famous ḍākinī Niguma presents four flaws that make it difficult to recognize mind's nature and which need to be overcome:

> Mind—the dharmakāya—lacks meeting and parting,
> but since it is too close, it is not recognized
> It dawns within but is too profound, ungrasped
> Though it is so simple, we do not trust it
> and thus we cannot remain undistracted
> Being so excellent, it doesn't fit into our mind
> Thus, we lack conviction and roam saṃsāra

Niguma also says in her song that the main practice of mahāmudrā consists of allowing these four flaws to be free in themselves. First, though our buddha nature (the dharmakāya) lacks any meeting or parting, it is not recognized, because it is too close. This is a little bit like trying to press our eye against the surface of a table to see it better. Doing so gets our eye as close to the table as it can possibly be, but it also means that we cannot see the table clearly. Rather than seeing all its details, because of being as close to it as we can be, we do not even recognize that it is a table, and on top of this, it hurts to do that. The way in which ordinary beings do not realize the nature of their mind is exactly like that: it is too close to be recognized, and the more they try to zoom in on it, the tighter their mind becomes, which hurts. This is why it is said that relaxation is important in the beginning, right from the point when we start with the view, and it is even more important in meditation and conduct. The Mahāmudrā tradition says that those people who can relax the best have the best meditation, those who relax in a medium manner have a medium meditation, and it is obvious what happens to those who cannot relax.

Second, though the nature of our mind is always present within us and even sends us wake-up calls all the time, it is not recognized, because it is too profound. It is not found in the ever-agitated waves on the surface of our busy dualistic mind with all its projections, but only in the depths of the vast ocean of mind's luminosity and emptiness.

Third, not only is the nature of our mind too close to be recognized, it is also too simple. Though, or rather because, it is completely simple, we do not trust it wholeheartedly, and that is the reason why we cannot remain undistracted from its simplicity. If someone says to us, "You are such a simple person," we usually do not take that as a compliment. But when we hear, "You are such a sophisticated person," we are very happy and feel appreciated. We usually are in love with sophistication. Nobody wants a simple iPhone 1 or 2 anymore; it must be the latest model, no matter how overpriced it is and no matter how few of its thousands of functions we actually use. Since our mind's nature is what is most simple, we don't get it and always keep looking for something more pompous.

Finally, our buddha nature is too excellent: it is too good to be true. Its infinite spaciousness, overwhelmingly brilliant awareness, and limitless qualities of awakening do not fit into our small and claustrophobic, dualistic minds; thus, since we only know the framework of our little narrow mind, we lack conviction in the boundless freedom of mahāmudrā and continue to roam saṃsāra.

A fable from India illustrates this nicely. A frog whose home was by the sea came to visit a frog who had lived at the bottom of a small well all his life, never having seen any larger body of water than the water in his own well. The frog in the well asked his visitor, "Where are you from?" "I live near the ocean." "What is that?" "It is an infinitely large body of water." "Hm, I doubt there is such a thing; at most it is maybe as big as a hundredth of the water in my well here." "No, no, it is much bigger!" "Well, maybe a tenth of the size of my well then?" "No, still much bigger!" "Okay, I'm really trying to stretch my imagination here—maybe it's half the size of my well?" "It's way beyond that!" "But it can't possibly be bigger than my entire well!" "It is by far, but if you don't believe me, come with me and I'll show you the ocean." The two frogs hopped to the coast, and once the ocean came into view, the frog from the sea pointed toward the endless waters stretching in front of them, saying, "See, *that* is the ocean!" When the frog from the well saw this infinity, he simply fainted because it blew his mind, being way beyond his wildest dreams about the possible size of a body of water.

Don't Look at the Finger, Look at the Moon

Milarepa's lines about the view say that with "**this wisdom of being empty, there is the danger of it getting lost in mere platitudes.**" Khenpo Rinpoche explains that no matter which nice or lofty terms for the nature of the mind we come up with, no matter how good they sound, no matter how excited they make us feel, that's not the wisdom Milarepa talks about. No matter how many times we say or think, "wisdom is empty," "wisdom is luminous," "wisdom is free from the duality of subject and object," "wisdom transcends the entirety of saṃsāra," "wisdom is the essence of all afflictions," "wisdom is the enlightened mind of all buddhas," it doesn't mean we actually experience or realize any of this, just as reading a recipe book does not make our hunger go away.

This is why Milarepa says that this nondual, nonconceptual wisdom free of all stains is in danger of becoming lost in merely blabbing about it. A lot of people talk and write about "the nature of the mind," "mind's luminosity," "buddha nature," "enlightenment," blah blah blah, just as I'm doing now, but that does not really mean anything. It only means something if we take these terms as being like fingers that point to something that is beyond those fingers. That is the only way in which such words can be useful. If we always get stuck on the fingers (some of them with a lot of nice rings, tattoos, or gloves), we will never see the moon at which those fingers are pointing. Thus, what Milarepa says here is, "Don't get stuck on the pointing fingers, but personally experience in your own mind what these fingers point to! Realize what these words refer to!"

If we look at the Buddha's teachings, we find many different teachings and a lot of different words for the same thing; there are many synonyms for pretty much everything. In this regard, it is interesting to look at the reports of what the Buddha said when he became the Awakened One. According to the *Lalitavistarasūtra*, he uttered this spontaneous verse:

> I have found this dharma that resembles nectar,
> profound, peaceful, nonreferential, luminous, and
>   unconditioned
> To whomever I would teach it could not understand it
> Thus, I shall just remain silent in the middle of the forest

And that is what the Buddha did for quite a while, indicating that nobody would understand what he had realized: this basic experience of mind's true nature. Later, however, he was encouraged by others to teach, and then he did nothing but that for the remaining forty-five years of his life. This may seem strange—how can he teach for forty-five years about something that, according to himself, nobody will understand anyway? As the Buddha said, his realization of the nature of the mind is inexpressible and inconceivable. However, that does not mean that this realization is completely inaccessible, which is a big difference. Though it is ultimately beyond words and thoughts, there still is a path that leads to eventually experiencing that very same realization in our own mind. It is still inconceivable, but our own experience of it is also inconceivable.

Possessing this insight, as well as the infinite compassion and capacity to actually show others how to reach mental freedom, the Buddha taught what cannot be taught. Obviously, we cannot experience the taste of some delicious food simply by hearing someone else talking about it. Still, we may become inspired by that talk to go shopping and prepare it in order to gain a firsthand experience of its taste. In the same way, we might become inspired to make an effort to taste the flavor of awakening by hearing or reading about it, without mistaking the words for its actual experience.

The Buddha taught the path to access this basic experience. He always said, "I cannot really make you a buddha, but I can teach you the path of how to get there, because I did it myself. However, it will be up to you to actually walk on that path." In fact, the Buddha always spoke from an experiential and practical point of view, no matter what he taught. He was down to earth and always emphasized our immediate experience of life, while discouraging mere philosophical or metaphysical speculations. Milarepa follows this by saying that we can talk about the nature of the mind for a long time, but if there is no experience of it from within, this is rather pointless. Not only that, even if we had some experience of the nature of the mind at some point, it can very easily become lost within all that talking about it. It may get buried within the jungle of our conceptual overlays, because usually we are more fascinated with those and our wish to share them than with our bare personal experience.

The next two lines of Milarepa's song say, "**If certainty about the heart of the matter does not arise, the clinging to a self will not become free through words.**" What we need to gain is firm certainty about what is actually meant when we talk about "the wisdom of being empty." Here, certainty does not just mean some words or thoughts that we may understand, such as what "the view" means, what "wisdom" means, what "empty" means, and how these words all hang together. That is a good start, but "certainty about the heart of the matter" refers to the certainty that arises from being in touch with a genuine experience of the ultimate nature of our mind. To have that experience represents definitive certainty. When we talk about the nature of the mind, we can have some conceptual understanding of what it is and what it is not and so on, but this is still like talking about some exotic Tibetan food that we have never tasted. No matter what we've been told, we really have no idea what it tastes like; we have to go get one and eat it. Only then can we be absolutely sure.

No Self, No Problem

Milarepa does not say that we should not gain a conceptual understanding of what he is talking about. However, any conceptual understanding, no matter how subtle or sophisticated it may be, needs to result in the incontrovertible personal certainty that is based on our very own experience and realization. If such certainty is not attained, words or concepts alone will not manage to free us from our clinging to a self. Therefore, Milarepa says that "**the keenest certainty is absolutely essential.**" In other words, the irreversible conviction that arises from within our personal experience is crucial. Conceptual talking or reasoning about things will not enable us to remove the root of our problems, which is the clinging to our precious self.

That can only happen if our fixation on "me" and "mine" is tackled on an experiential and habitual level, because that grasping is a deeply ingrained experience. It is not just an idea, like "I'm John" or "I'm Mary," which is merely the most superficial level of such clinging. The more deep-seated clinging to ourselves as individual distinct beings happens on an instinctive or gut level. We can almost call it some form of survival instinct. Even animals have it, which shows in their many ways of trying to protect themselves from threats and create conducive conditions for their survival and well-being. According to the Buddhist teachings, this basic clinging to "me"—seeing ourselves as individuals that are separate from others and behaving accordingly—is the fundamental root of our suffering. If we do not gain certainty in the basic experience of the nature of the mind, which is completely without any kind of self, we will not be able to remove our fixation on our self.

So why is the clinging to a self a problem? It sounds pretty normal and everybody does it, so what is wrong with it? We seem to need it to find our way in the world among others and to make correct decisions that benefit us. That we all have and cherish our own self is really a majority decision, so it must be right, no? The problem with our clinging to a self is that it is the starting point of all our disturbing thoughts, emotions, afflictions, and the ensuing suffering.

In the vast spaciousness of mind's nature, just as it is, there is no reference point whatsoever, let alone any kind of a single, lasting, and independent self or ego. Mind's basic expanse of wakeful luminosity is like the clear bright sky without a single cloud. However, it is precisely this infinitely vast openness of mind's nature, in which there is nothing to hold on to and no ground to stand on, that makes us freak out. In order to feel more secure or grounded, we try to cling to something where there isn't really anything to hold on to, and this illusory and self-made "something" is what we take to be our self. Out of fear of our mind's overwhelming open-endedness and spaciousness, we try to establish a completely artificial reference point where there is no reference point at all. In fact, we are desperately trying to hold on to nothing, since the self does not exist, but it is exactly the effort that this holding on requires that makes us feel as if we are holding on to something. That is called "clinging to a self."

It is similar to clenching our fist and feeling that we are actually holding on to something. However, if we clench our fist very hard, the sense of holding on to something becomes eclipsed by our feeling of pain. Obviously, the remedy for that is neither taking a painkiller nor cutting off our hand—the remedy is to simply relax our tight grip and uncurl our fingers. Likewise, we need to let go of our tight self-involvedness and realize that there is nothing to hold on to and that any attempt of "pulling ourselves together" will just hurt us more.

As long as we entertain this clinging to our self, there is automatically a notion of "other," which is everything and everybody we do not hold on to as being "us." Within that "other," there are some persons or things that we like and wish to incorporate into the territory of our own Planet Ego, as well as some that we do not like and want to get rid of. Through this desire of wanting to adopt some phenomena (attachment) and wanting to reject others (aversion), we are propelled into committing certain actions to get what we want and to get rid of what we do not want. All of these actions have corresponding results, which are more or less pleasant or unpleasant, thus giving rise to various forms of happiness and suffering. In this way, we keep spinning in the vicious circle of conditioned existence that Buddhists call "saṃsāra."

Once we are in the middle of our everyday struggles and pain, there is no way that we could be aware that it all started (and restarts every moment anew) with our clinging to what does not exist, our holding on to nothing. From a buddha's point of view, our clinging to a self is a complete fiction, a weird fantasy, a fixed idea. This clinging is the root of the entire colorful tree of our saṃsāric existence, with its firm trunk of taking everything to be so solid, its limitless branches of our endless and pointless activities, its lush leaves of our thick concepts and belief systems, its dazzling blossoms of our precious emotions, and its bittersweet fruits of our illusory happiness and suffering. Therefore, since the clinging to our self is the root of all our resulting troubles and suffering, the Buddha said that this is what we need to relinquish in order to realize what is actually going on and free ourselves from the self-spun cocoon of attachment, aversion, and ignorance.

What Is My Mind without Me?

As Milarepa says here, the nature of the mind, just as it is, is the only thing that is completely free from any self-clinging. So the big question here is, "What is my mind without me?" Can we imagine that? If someone asks us, "What is your mind without you?" what do we answer?

Usually, we do not grant our mind any right of existing on its own. We treat it like a dog—"my dog," "my mind": it's the same thing. Maybe even worse, because usually we treat our dog better than we treat our mind. Our mind is more like a slave to us, whom we assign all kinds of tasks. We never leave our mind alone, we never give it the space to be a mind in, to just be as it is on its own. We never give it any vacation days; luckily for us, our mind has not joined any labor union either, otherwise we would be in trouble. Maybe our mind has a bit of leeway when we are asleep, dream, or daydream, but otherwise it's pretty much always under pressure.

From this perspective, the "view" here means to take the lid off of that pressure cooker called "clinging to a self," release some steam, and let our mind stretch a bit. Then, since we're not bugging it all the time, we can venture into looking at what our mind is doing. What does it do on its own? This is why Milarepa says that definitive certainty that comes from within is so important. If we at least get a glimpse of what "my mind without me" is, it means a great deal, because then there is suddenly a lot of space and a lot of fresh air. There are dimensions and experiences that we never had before and never thought possible.

The big question is how we may gain such certainty, since it is so important according to Milarepa. How can we experience the nature of the mind and be really certain about that? Ultimately speaking, if we wonder what a buddha is like, the only way to really find out is to become one; only then can we be sure.

Practically speaking, there are basically two ways to get there. Plan A is to receive a pointing-out instruction that introduces the nature of our mind from a qualified teacher and directly recognize what is pointed out or introduced. Plan B is to go through a more progressive approach, which does not exclude pointing-out instructions, but serves as a preparation and mental background for them. This gradual approach is known as "the progressive stages of meditation on emptiness." Besides being of course considered essential in all schools of Mahāyāna Buddhism, substantial study of emptiness is specifically required in certain parts of the Kagyü and Nyingma schools before practitioners are introduced to the actual meditations of mahāmudrā and dzogchen.

When we look at Milarepa's line "**With the view, which is this wisdom of being empty**," we can understand this in the light of these progressive stages of meditation on emptiness. Be it in the Mahāyāna in general or the Mahāmudrā and Dzogchen traditions in particular, it is crucial to gain a sound understanding of emptiness by gradually eliminating more and more misconceptions about ourselves and all phenomena, including emptiness itself. More specifically, we need to undermine and eventually overcome our clinging to a really existent personal self, as well as to the real existence of phenomena other than our self.

Usually, even among Buddhists, emptiness does not receive good press. When hearing the word "emptiness," most people think of some-thing like an empty glass, an empty house, an empty wallet, an empty bank account, an empty fridge, or simply totally empty space. We have a strong tendency to think of "emptiness" in the sense of lacking some-thing (or everything), or simply utter nothingness. But that is not at all what the Buddha meant by emptiness. In fact, just like existence or rei-fication, nonexistence or nothingness is one of the main mistaken refer-ence points that are to be relinquished by the proper understanding of emptiness.

As a Buddhist philosophical concept or technical term, "emptiness" refers to all phenomena being without any intrinsic nature or core of their own, or their assumed real and solid existence being completely unfindable under analysis. However, in terms of the actual experience of this kind of emptiness, it means nothing other than complete mental freedom, openness, spaciousness, relaxation, a lot of fresh air, a lot of lightness, a lot of room for all kinds of things to manifest, and a lot of good-hearted humor; it seems nobody can really complain about that. Thus, in the "progressive stages of meditation on emptiness," we are not dealing so much with philosophical or theoretical analysis but rather with using increasingly refined conceptual scrutiny in order to allow for the spaciousness, relaxation, and serenity of the state of mind of directly experiencing and realizing what emptiness is like.

This progression begins with the most fundamental Buddhist approach of the śrāvakas, which speaks about the absence or emptiness of a personal self.[4] There are many detailed explanations on how to med-itate on or get used to the fact that there is no self anywhere in our body, our mind, our thoughts, our feelings, or any other part of us. In a nutshell though, there are basically two approaches.

First, we may compare all the various parts of our body and mind with what we spontaneously or experientially feel our self to be. We simply ask ourselves questions such as "Is my head my self?" "Do I take my mind to be my self?" "Are my emotions my self?" "Which one of them?" "Are my body and mind controlled by my self? If so, how?" Usually, we do not feel that our self is limited to only our body or any of its parts. This simply is not our experience of "me." However, when it comes to our mind or our emotions, the answer may not be that simple. We could ask ourselves, "If my mind is my self, how exactly is that so?" "Is it my entire mind or just a certain part of it?" "Does this correspond to my experience of 'me' in all situations?" By proceeding in that way, we will inevitably come upon the crucial question that we should have asked at the beginning of our search: "What exactly is my self?"

This leads to the second, more systematic and thorough, approach of investigation. In general, to compare two things, we must know what each of them is. We cannot really compare our body and mind with our self if we do not know what this self is. Thus, the next step is to try to define or describe our self. This process in itself is already very illuminating in determining whether this self actually exists or not. For, apart from a definite "feeling" that we have a self, most people have a very hard time coming up with an exact description of what this self or "I" might be. Paradoxically, one of the main reasons we are convinced that we have a self is that we don't really know exactly what it is or what it looks like. Since our sense of a self is so vague, it is open to virtually any projection or identification. Actually, we constantly shift the objects on which we build this idea of a self. Sometimes we relate it more to our body, sometimes more to our thoughts, sometimes to our emotions, sometimes to our career, and so on. We tend to say things such as "I am sick" as well as "My head hurts," "I am a lawyer," "I think," "There are too many thoughts in my mind," "I am sad," or "My depression has worsened." All of these statements expose different ways of assuming and relating to an underlying self, yet we usually do not see their contradictory nature. Therefore, we constantly take the existence of some underlying "I" somewhere in our body or mind for granted and refer to it as such.

The basic meditation here is to mentally go through all the many coarse and subtle elements of our psycho-physical existence (also known as the five skandhas) and gain certainty that none of them is a self that in some way is single, lasting, and independent (or in control). It's easy to start with our big toe, for example. Obviously, when asked directly, nobody would identify their big toe as their self; but when we bump this toe against something hard and it hurts, experientially, it seems very much to be the place where our self is, so there is some room for investigation.

What we try to see here is that there is really nothing but our body and our mind, and no self or ego on top of them that possesses them, controls them, or has any other kind of relationship with them. The more we can see that our body and mind are working perfectly well on their own, that they do not need any self or ego, and are in fact better off without one, the more we see that this self is as redundant as a fifth wheel on a car. It is not only redundant; it also disturbs and sabotages our body and mind from operating smoothly and naturally on their own, just like sand in our gearshift or an overblown antivirus program messing with our other software.

More details on this and the following steps of the progressive stages of meditation on emptiness can be found in Khenpo Tsultrim Gyamtso Rinpoche's book *The Progressive Stages of Meditation on Emptiness*.

Mind Is on Its Own

The following four steps in this progression all deal with the emptiness of phenomena other than our self.

The second step is what is called "the Mind-Only or Cittamātra approach." Once we have realized that there is no personal self anywhere within our body and mind, we are still stuck with our mind, so what about it? Even after we realize that there is no actual self, there is still something that experiences and something that is experienced, a basic sense of dualism of object and subject. For example, when we see a tree, experientially the perceiver seems to be somewhere here within our body, while the tree seems to be out there. The same goes for the rest of our sense perceptions. Even when we think, there is a difference between the thinking mind and what it thinks about. This felt sense of subject and object being different is not just a concept but the natural way in which our dualistic mind is hardwired when it operates and interacts with objects. In other words, there always seems to be a gap between subject and object.

The meditation here is to see whether there really is a difference between the perceiver and the perceived, or whether both are simply different appearances within the mind. The point is that, from the point of view of our direct experience, whether it is an object or the experiencer of that object, it is all just something that appears in our mind, because we can never step out of our mind and check what the world would look like if it were not perceived by us. That's why it is said in the Mind-Only approach that "the world" is nothing but what appears as this world within our mind. That means what appears in our mind makes up our world and what appears in someone else's mind makes up their world. We can only talk about "the world" in terms of what appears and what we perceive in our own mind, and we can never experience what others experience. Thus, no experience of any two people is ever the same. From that point of view, whatever we experience is necessarily always something that appears solely to our own mind, whether we like it or not. Therefore, there is no real difference between what appears in our mind as perceiver and what appears as perceived, because both are just facets of our mind.

In this second stage of meditation on emptiness, the existence of objects as anything other than mental experiences is negated. That is, we examine the seeming difference or distance between mind and its objects, for example by asking ourselves questions such as, "Where is the borderline between my mind and its objects?" "Does the perceiver go out to meet the object or does the object come in?" "If either is the case, how far would the mind have to go out or how far would the object have to come in?" "Apart from feeling that what appears as a chair over there is something outside, what proofs are there for it actually existing outside of my perception of it?" "If mind and matter are different, how exactly do they meet?"

More systematically, the lack of truly existent objects is analyzed in three ways: (1) by breaking them down into infinitely smaller parts, (2) by analyzing the object and its perception on a causal timeline, and (3) by seeing the subjectivity of every appearance and experience.

1. The issue of whether there are any really existing outer objects can be approached in a way that is very similar to that of modern physics:

breaking up these objects into smaller and smaller parts without find-ing any indivisible final core. If there is no findable, substantial core to external objects, we must conclude that what we experience as outer objects are nothing but a projection or image in our mind, just as in a dream, when we also seem to experience outer objects while clearly there are none.

2. We can also focus on whether there is any causal relation between objects and our perception of them. In terms of our own perception, we can only speak about the existence of an object once we actually perceive it in one way or another. As long as we do not perceive it, we have no way of directly knowing whether there is such an object. Thus, it is obvious that what appears as an object to our perception and that perception itself invariably occur simultaneously. If there were actual outer objects that exist external to our mind and serve as the causes for our percep-tion of them, they would have to exist before the perceptions that are their results, for causes must precede their results in time and also cease as soon as these results arise. But if these outer objects existed before our perception of them, what would we perceive, since these objects are already gone at the time this perception arises?

3. If we consider what exactly we know of objects, we see that every perception is only a subjective experience in our mind as the perceiver. If we touch or smell a rose, its "softness" or its "fragrance" is really nothing but our experience of softness or fragrance. This accords well with what cognitive science says: there is no "objective" softness and fragrance of anything apart from what we subjectively experience as such. There are no objects outside of the mind, because our perceptions and what they perceive are alike in that they are nothing but immaterial clear appear-ances in our mind. In other words, objects are not different from the cognizing consciousness because of the very fact that they are cogniza-ble and cognized. Consciousness—lucid awareness that neither con-sists of particles nor has any spatial extension—can only cognize that which has the same nature as consciousness, not some assumed material objects that have an altogether different nature or definition (such as being what lacks cognizance, consists of particles, and possesses spatial dimensions). Hence, again, objects in a dream and in the waking state

are not fundamentally different. Both seem to perform their functions in their respective contexts, but none of them really exists as something separate from our experience.

This is not to deny that the objects of our perceptions *appear* to us as if they existed externally. However, apart from the fact that they subjectively appear this way, there is no evidence that there really are external objects in any way other than what appears as such objects in the mind. The most common example for this is again appearances in a dream: we can have the same experiences as in waking life, such as seemingly external material objects that seem to be different from our dream body and dream mind. However, despite appearing to be external, it is clear that these dream objects never existed anywhere else but only as appearances in our own dreaming mind. Therefore, whether in a dream or in the waking state, the mere fact that something *appears as if* being outside is no proof that it actually does exist outside of our mind.

In brief, if there are no really existent objects, there are no really existent corresponding subjects that perceive them either. However, since mind is not just nothingness but full of experience, awareness, and dynamic activity, the result of this step of "Mind-Only" is to simply rest within the bare experience that is empty of any sense of dualism of subject and object. Within mere experience or sheer lucid awareness, there is not only no self, there is no notion of duality of subject and object either.

Do We Find Our Mind?

Even if we realize that there are neither really existent objects nor subjects to perceive them, there is still the subtle clinging to the reality of mere experience, free from perceiver and perceived. Therefore, the third stage, called "the Svātantrika-Madhyamaka approach," deals with looking into the nature of mind's experience without a personal self or duality. As long as we do not analyze the nature of this sheer experience, it is clear and vivid; it is right there. But once we analyze it, we cannot really find it.

For example, if we eat a piece of chocolate, we cannot deny the experience of eating and tasting it, but if we try to pinpoint the experience and say that it is exactly like this or that, we cannot really find it. Therefore, it is said that this experience appears but in fact it is empty: it lacks any real and solid existence of its own—there is no true core to it that can be found anywhere. This does not mean that there is no experience at all; nobody can deny that there is obviously some process of experiencing going on. However, when we try to nail down what exactly it is, there is nothing to be found. That is why, in a famous Zen quote, a master asks his student the following question:

> I have something: When I do not look for it, it is there. When I look for it, it is not there. What is it?

In our meditation here, we can analyze nondual experience by asking questions: "What is this experience actually?" "Can we pinpoint it as something?" "Does it have any size, shape, or color?" "Is my experience of seeing a blue square blue and square?" "Where does that experience come from, where does it abide, and where does it cease?" "How does that experience arise, how does it exit, and how does it perish?" "Is it inside the body?" "Is it outside?"

In a more systematic and stringent way, we can analyze our lucid momentary experience through the five great Madhyamaka reasonings (such as whether it arises from itself, something else, both, or neither) and so on, arriving at the conclusion that it, like all other phenomena, is empty of any intrinsic nature of its own.

So far, starting with our personal self, we found neither any objects outside of the mind, nor any perceiving subjects, nor a bare experience free from the duality of subject and object. This unfindability of all phenomena, or the absence of an inherent, real nature of all phenomena, is the object as well as the result of our meditation in this third stage here. Technically speaking, being empty of a nature of its own or being completely unfindable is called "a nonimplicative negation, which is similar to space." Not having found any phenomena, including mind's nondual experience, we let mind relax and rest in its very own unfindability, which is similar to empty space.

Letting Go of Everything

The fourth stage of meditation is called "the Prāsaṅgika-Madhyamaka approach." The manner of analysis here is pretty much the same as in the third stage. However, having analyzed our experience and not found it, we rest in that state of space-like nonfinding, but there is still some clinging to that unfindability. In other words, the notion of emptiness in the sense of the absence of a real nature is still a subtle reference point. In the fourth approach, we try to let go of that reference point as well. So we can see that this process is becoming more and more subtle. The clinging to the unfindability of our experience under analysis is a very subtle form of clinging, much subtler than clinging to a self or to subject and object. The clinging here is not to "something" but to not finding any "something." Therefore, what we do here is not to conduct any additional analysis over and above stage three. Rather, once we haven't found anything under analysis, we try to let go of any further analysis or any holding on within the state of nonfinding, including holding on to this very state of nonfinding.

This is called "the emptiness of being free from all reference points" or "the emptiness of being completely nondiscursive." It means to be free from anything to solidify, reify, or cling to, no matter whether it is external, internal, subject, object, sheer experience, or the unfindability of sheer experience, including "being free from all reference points." In other words, in order for our mind to be able to fully relax within its ultimate expanse, free from any center or limit, it has to let go of even its most subtle grasping at any reference point, including the very lack of any reference points. This is the vast and open spaciousness of experiencing the actual freedom from all discursiveness that is the result of the fourth step.

Relishing the Taste of Letting Go

As for the fifth level of the progressive stages of meditation on emptiness, which is called "Shentong-Madhyamaka," we may wonder what could come after that fourth one of having let go of everything and not having any reference points at all. From the point of view of those who regard the fourth stage as the final view and meditation, it is said that there is nothing beyond it. However, there are others who say that this kind of totally letting go of everything could still be slightly problematic, if we work with it as a habitual pattern of always saying, "This is not it, that is not it, and this one is not it either," no matter what we experience. If that habit of constantly eliminating any reference point turns into a dismissal of any experience in our mind, we might even dismiss the actual experience of the nature of the mind, thinking, "This is not it either," which in a sense brings us back to square one.

Thus, at the fifth level of meditation on emptiness, we still rest in the fourth state of having totally let go of everything, but we focus slightly more on the experience of having let go completely. In other words, we relax our mind completely and then experience both its relaxation and its luminous wakefulness. This is called "emptiness and luminosity inseparable."

Since the utter freedom from discursiveness and reference points described in the last step is not just some blank space or mere absence (which would be a form of extinction or nihilism), it is also described here as luminosity or "the unity of wisdom and expanse." Hence, in terms of the actual nature of mind, the fifth stage is not an additional or higher stage above the freedom from discursiveness. As Sakya Paṇḍita says in his *Distinction of the Three Vows*, the very attempt to go higher or beyond the actual freedom from all reference points would inevitably create a new reference point, thus falling out of the state of nonreferentiality. Thus, the fourth and fifth stages indicate the two aspects of the nature of our mind, which is the undifferentiable unity of the freedom from reference points and luminosity.

When we just talk about this progression, in a sense, it seems to be going backward. Before, during the third and fourth stages, we already understood that there is no experiencer, not even a findable experience. Now, in the fifth stage, we are told to focus more on the experience of what the fourth stage is like. However, at this point, this is a different level of experience altogether. The experience of having let go completely of everything yet being fully aware of that is different from any ordinary dualistic experience. That's why Milarepa says "**there is the danger of it getting lost in mere platitudes.**" Particularly on the subtler levels of these progressive stages, the main point is not to theorize or conceptualize, but to personally experience what is described. Whatever else someone may say or think is just like a pointing finger.

When Milarepa speaks here of "**the wisdom of being empty,**" he refers to that fifth stage of the progressive stages of emptiness. The "empty" aspect of "wisdom" in terms of what is absent from that wisdom is what we practice with in the first four stages, as we let go of more and more things that we cling too, such as our self, subject, object, any findable kind of experience, and even the reference point of "being without any reference point." We drop all of these. Nevertheless, beyond that empty aspect of wisdom, there is still the underlying stream of *experiencing* letting go of everything. There is a basic awareness of experiencing that there is no self. There is a basic awareness of experiencing that there is no duality. Likewise, it is basic awareness that experiences the lack of any reference point. However, when mind realizes its nature as being free from all reference points, that does not mean we drop dead or dissolve into a vacuum. That is obviously not the point, nor would it be very inspiring: if that were the outcome of this kind of meditation, it would be hard to motivate anybody to do it. The point is to see that even when the mind is completely free from anything to hold on to (including itself), there is still this experiential quality of it not holding on to anything, but this is a level of experience that is beyond any dualistic state of mind.

In summary, we could outline the progression of meditating on emptiness in these five steps as follows. We start with meditating on and realizing the lack of a personal self. Then, in terms of the lack of real existence of all phenomena, we progress from overcoming the coarse notion of real objects through the subtler notion of mere nondual consciousness. In turn, this sense of a mere nondual consciousness is relinquished by resting in emptiness as the sheer unfindability of anything. Finally, mind is simply let be in its natural state of nonreferential spacious freedom, while at the same time being unconditionally aware of its own radiant display.

The subtle reference point that is still entertained at the third stage of this progression is the clinging to the observation that there is nothing to be found (that being the realization at this point). We do not find our mind and we do not find anything else either, so we think, "There is nothing to be found whatsoever, that's it," which is still a sort of tagline. The fourth stage means to let go of that tagline too, in whatever form it may appear. At that point, we might think or feel that there is no reference point whatsoever, but that is just another reference point. So we have to let go of that too. This is part of the process on the fourth stage: letting go of anything we hold on to, whatever it is, even any subtle holding on to not holding on to anything. The fifth stage is not really different from the fourth one: they are like two sides of the same coin. The fourth stage is the culmination of the process of letting go of everything, but just letting go completely is not the full experiential scope of the nature of the mind, because the mind also has its innate qualities, such as vivid wakefulness, awareness, luminosity, compassion, and wisdom. These natural qualities of our mind shine forth in an unimpeded manner when it finally lets go of its most fundamental layer of being uptight.

For example, in the sky without any clouds, birds, airplanes, and so on, there are no reference points whatsoever; there is no south, north, west, or east. However, during daytime that sky is not only devoid of all these things, it also has a quality of utter all-pervasive brightness and luminosity. Likewise, the fifth stage means to focus on or simply experience mind's natural luminosity, but always within, or inseparable from, its infinite spaciousness of having let go and being completely relaxed and at ease. This is very different from conceptualizing, fantasizing, or just becoming excited about that prospect.

It is this radically different level of experience that is the main point in Buddhist approaches such as Mahāmudrā, Dzogchen, and the Vajrayāna. Fundamentally, they all deal with the level of having already let go of all reference points and then looking at what that experience is like. We can talk about "no reference points" as being like an object, but if there is no experience of that "object," there is no realization either. For example, a table is also free from reference points, it never entertains any, but that is not what we call "buddhahood." Therefore, "freedom from reference points" is not something in the abstract; it refers to the mind's *experience* of being free from reference points.

This is precisely what Milarepa talks about when he says, "**the view, which is this wisdom of being empty**." Thus, "the view" here refers to the basic experience of the nature of the mind, which is empty of everything else that is not this experience: that is, all our coarse and subtle concepts about what the nature of the mind may or may not be. This means that this "wisdom of being empty" is also empty of everything that Buddhism says about it, because all those statements are likewise just concepts that point to it. As Milarepa says, in the end, all appearances are buddha: the mind is the Buddha and whatever appears in the mind is a buddha realm.

In the approaches of Mahāmudrā, Dzogchen, and the Vajrayāna, this can be experienced in any moment. That is the good thing about it, because it is our mind, and our mind is always there. Of course, this experience of our mind is not a given, but a lot of people actually do glimpse it once in a while; they just don't know what it is. That's why it is said that it is good, through at least some study, to get a better idea of what it is and what it is not. Of course, it is even better if we have a qualified teacher who can point us in the right direction or say, "That's not it." But in the end, it needs to be realized by our own mind without anyone else pointing it out: we have to follow the fingers and then see for ourselves. That is possible in any moment, like right now. It is important to remember that we are not talking about something out there; it is our own mind, which is the closest there is. It is very difficult to realize, because it is so close (as in the example of pressing our eye against a table). But on the other hand, it is also easy, maybe too easy. So a lot of it has to do with not doing anything or trying to get it, but undoing what we usually do, because what obscures our mind's nature is all our doing; that's what we are really good at. How do we do undoing? Well, that's the tricky point, we cannot "do" undoing. There is no twelve-step program to realize the nature of the mind, saying, first, you do this and then this and then *boom*.

There are many stories about highly unlikely situations in which people's ordinary state of mind became "undone" and something else happened. My favorite one is about a monk going to the monastery's outhouse. In Tibet, that just means some shed at the edge of a cliff with a hole in the floor, so whatever is produced just drops down the cliff. When that monk was in the outhouse, his teacher sneaked up to its closed door and even brought all the other monks of the monastery as well as all the people from the neighboring village. They were all standing in a big crowd in front of that outhouse when the teacher suddenly opened its door. The monk was squatting there, not with his pants down, but his robes down, and first became completely shocked at the door being opened and hundreds of people staring at him. When he snapped out of his shock, he pulled up his robes and got extremely angry at his teacher. He was holding his robes with one hand and chasing the teacher across the courtyard of the monastery. The teacher was running in front and the student was chasing after him, shouting, "I'm going to kill you; why did you do this?" As they kept running, the monk kept insulting and shouting at his teacher, becoming angrier and angrier. Eventually, the monk got closer and closer to his teacher and when he had almost caught up with him and tried to grab him, the teacher stopped, turned around, and pointed at the monk's face, saying, "Now look at your mind!" And that was that. So maybe that is the twelve-step program.

APPEARANCE AND EMPTINESS: WHY CAN'T THEY JUST GET ALONG?[5]

Let's briefly go through some other songs of Milarepa that also speak about the view, further elucidating what he says in his *Ultimate View, Meditation, Conduct, and Fruition*. In fact, most of Milarepa's songs comment on each other, so they are both songs to be commented on and commentaries on other songs. The first song we will look at is called *Eight Kinds of Mastery*, and its first two lines present the view as follows:

> When appearance and emptiness are inseparable,
> this represents the mastery of the view[6]

Without thinking about Buddhist philosophy, what comes to our mind spontaneously when we hear the word "appearance"? Usually we think that there is something there, being more or less real. We think about something existent. On the other hand, what do we think when we hear "emptiness"? We think of the opposite—nothing being there. So what does Milarepa mean by saying, "When appearance and emptiness are inseparable," considering these two to be indivisible or undifferentiable? It sounds like he is talking about having existence and nonexistence in the same place. Like something is both there and not there. Does that make sense? Is there an example of something that is there and not there? We could say that a table in a dream is there and not there: it is there when we dream and it is not there when we wake up. But that is not what Milarepa is talking about here. He is not speaking about something that first appears and then is gone, which refers to different times. What he is saying is that appearance and emptiness are a unity simultaneously, always being inseparable. This is exactly the same as what the *Heart Sūtra*'s most famous passage says:

> Form is emptiness. Emptiness is form. Emptiness is no other than form and form is no other than emptiness.

But again, what does that mean apart from the mere words? In order to "master the view," as Milarepa says, the point is not to separate those two—appearance and emptiness. How do we do that? Fundamentally, by getting used to the fact that this is the way things are, which, in Buddhism, we call study, reflection, and meditation. We analyze phenomena through going into our mental lab, just like scientists going into the big underground roller coasters where they smash up subatomic particles. That's one way to do it, but it's a bit expensive, and they do not let everybody in there. The other way to do it is through our own experience and investigation. First, we come to some understanding of what the inseparability of appearance and emptiness means, and then we develop certainty about it. Finally, we meditate on it, which means becoming familiar with it and used to it.

Now, if we look at the physicists with their particle accelerators, they smash particles every day while knowing very well that even those particles do not really exist and that, fundamentally, phenomena just consist of a lot of space with a little bit of energy floating around within it. But does that influence the way they behave in everyday life? No, because once their exciting day in the lab with all their new discoveries is over, they close the lab's door, which does not really exist. They walk on their nonexistent feet on some nonexistent ground. They go to their nonexistent car, drive on a nonexistent road, arrive at their nonexistent house, and eat some nonexistent hamburgers. In other words, they do not behave as if everything is mostly space, though they know it.

In Buddhism, we take a different approach in that we try to gain an experience of what all that actually means for our behavior and how it changes our entire outlook about ourselves and the world. When we do not separate the facts of all phenomena appearing yet being empty (that is, not existing as they appear), it is like what Milarepa says in the second stanza of his song here:

> When dreams and daytime are not different,
> this represents the mastery of meditation

That means to first gain an understanding that whatever appears is not really different from how dream appearances arise: they appear but do not really exist. Therefore, "appearance" in Buddhism does not mean really or solidly existing. It simply means appearing in a way that is like what appears in a movie, a rainbow, a dream, or an illusion. That also explains the emptiness part in it, which is the fact that whatever appears does not really exist. At the same time, nobody can deny that there are mere temporary and fleeting appearances. This is the understanding of not separating the two. It is not that things first are really existent and then, when we understand that, they do not really exist anymore, having become empty. They always have been, always are, and always will be empty of real existence, no matter in what form, in what intensity, or for how long they appear; we just do not realize that.

For example, we may have the experience of looking for a certain pen on our big writing desk, which is full of all kinds of pens, papers, files, and other things. We look for this pen and we know exactly what it looks like and that it must be on our desk, but we do not see it. We look over the desk many times and, despite the pen sitting right there, we still do not see it. This is like looking at the world: emptiness is right in front of our nose all the time, but we just do not see emptiness. It is not something that has to be newly introduced; it is there all the time. Thus, emptiness is not some kind of sublime metaphysic concept or some abstract truth or law of the universe. In terms of appearances, emptiness is simply the basic fact that whatever appears does not exist on its own; rather, everything is contingent on many other things, which is called "dependent origination." If we try to find something that exists on its own, by its own nature, inherently, or independently, we cannot find such a thing, and yet we constantly perceive all kinds of fleeting appearances. In fact, Buddhism says that it is precisely because things are empty, which means not being solid, independent, and unchanging, that anything can appear or change. If everything really existed in a fixed and solid way, nothing could ever change. The universe would be frozen in its first moment of appearance or never appear at all. We too would always be the same. In other words, from the Buddhist point of view, the very fact that things appear and change is a clear sign of emptiness or the lack of any solid, independent, and intrinsic existence. When we understand that and gain some experience in it, this is "the mastery of the view."

Next, let's look at Milarepa's song *The Profound Definitive Meaning Sung on the Snowy Range*. Its first four lines say:

> In the mind with the view, emptiness dawns
> There's not even a speck of an essence of what is to be
>   viewed
> A viewer and what is viewed are undone and gone
> This way of realizing the view is excellent[7]

Milarepa says, "In the mind with the view, emptiness dawns" but "there's not even a speck of an essence of what is to be viewed." When the view is mastered as it is understood here, there is not just some understanding of emptiness but a direct personal experience of what that means. In whatever we see, whatever we hear, whatever we perceive, whatever we think, there is not even an atom of substantial reality. Let alone anything material, there is also nothing in the nature of our mind—what is to be viewed ultimately—that we can pinpoint. Nor is there anything that we can isolate as the experience of that nature. Thus, since neither "a viewer and what is viewed" are findable, they "are undone and gone." This means that the subject-object duality that we usually always experience—such as "me" and "others," perceiver and perceived, inner and outer—also vanishes. There are no such distinctions anymore.

We have a hard time even imagining a perception without a subject and object, because it is a very ingrained habit. Usually, we think that there is a "me" who perceives and there are objects perceived by this "me," which are different. Here, Milarepa speaks about there being no difference between object and subject, so we cannot draw any borderline or boundary between those two. Usually, we draw these boundaries, like taking a table to be an outside object. That table is clearly not the perceiver: if we ask anybody, "Is this table the perceiver?" the answer will be "no." Whether we think that our mind is the perceiver, our self, or whatever, it is very clear that we do not think that the perceiver is the table (or anything else "out there"): the table is what is perceived. So, how does it feel if there is no difference between the perceiver and the table? Do we feel offended by that? Does that mean we are the same as the table? Or is the table part of us? When Milarepa speaks about the difference between subject and object falling away, it means that whatever is experienced is just something that appears in the mind, no matter whether it appears to be the perceiving aspect of the mind or the perceived aspect of the mind.

When it is realized that things are not truly existing, the notion of truly existing subjects and objects dissolves as well. This is a basic part of the deal with emptiness. Thus, Milarepa continues, "This way of realizing the view is excellent." It seems that at least it worked for him. Though it may sound like it, all this does not mean that there is just some vast space with nothing left after everything has dissolved. Remember the first two lines in the last song: there is still appearance, so understanding and realizing emptiness does not at all mean that things simply disappear completely. (Fortunately or unfortunately, depending on the things . . .) The most common misunderstanding about emptiness is to think that it means utter nonexistence. Therefore, Milarepa speaks about the union or the inseparability of appearance and emptiness.

Waking Up from Our Own Dream

In other words, with an understanding of emptiness, things still appear, but we do not take them so seriously anymore. We do not have such a heavy-handed approach to them. If we think about how we deal experientially with dream appearances after we have woken up, as opposed to how we deal with the appearances of so-called real life, we can see the difference. Once we realize that something is just a dream, even if it was very awful, we can let it go and stop suffering from it. We might still have a bad morning after a nightmare, but eventually we get over it the more it sinks in that what appeared in our nightmare did not really happen. On the other hand, whatever may happen during the day, we usually solidify it more and more. We do not solidify our dreams very much (unless we do dream analysis), but we greatly solidify our waking life, sometimes even after many years, thinking things like, "I remember exactly what he or she said or did at that time and I'm still angry about it."

Again, emptiness does not mean nothingness or some blank and void space. It means that appearances still appear and our experiences still happen, but our way of dealing with them is different, more light-handed. We stop taking everything to be so heavy and serious. We could say that the experience of emptiness shows itself in people through the attitudes of being relaxed and not so humorless. Maybe that's why great masters laugh so much.

Our next song is Milarepa's *Three Nails*:

> When the three nails of the view are explained,
> all possible appearances are contained in the mind
> Mind as such is in the natural state of luminosity
> Within that, there is nothing to be identified[8]

In this song, Milarepa is working as a carpenter of mind, it seems. He hammers three nails each into view, meditation, conduct, and fruition, driving home three key points of each. In terms of the view, the first nail or crucial point is that "all possible appearances are contained in the mind." In other words, whatever appears is nothing but something that appears in the mind. This is not to be misunderstood in the sense that this table, for example, literally is or consists of mind when we see it; otherwise, that table would have or be consciousness. What it means is that whatever appears—no matter whether it seems to be outside or inside, matter or mind, ourselves or other beings—is nothing other than an appearance in our minds. We cannot really know any hypothetical or generic world outside of the one that is perceived by our mind. We cannot do comparative studies about a world that exists independently from our own perception of it. Nor can we step out of our own mind and experience what other people experience. We are always stuck with nothing but our own experience. To us, it may seem from the outside that certain other people have a happier or more miserable life than us, but we have no way of experiencing what is actually going on in their mind.

From this Buddhist point of view, not only is there no common external world that is just seen differently by different beings, there is no independently existing external world at all. Instead, everyone has their own movie about their own world going on in their own mind. However, since all those movies are pretty similar, at least for humans, humans usually agree that they perceive the same things (unless we ask ten witnesses about what happened at a crime scene and get ten different answers). This is also why we can talk about our experiences and it seems that other people understand us. However, even on a conventional level, more often than not, this image of commonality falls apart once we realize that we have perceived what we think of as "the same thing," "the same event," or "the same person" in radically different ways, or that others do not understand us at all. Then we keep arguing with others about how things really are, which is, of course, always our own version of how things are. In other words, all our experiences and what appears to us are completely individual and unique. They are solely our own experience: at any given moment, nobody's experience is ever the same as anyone else's. Nor are a single person's experiences in different moments ever the same.

Confused Mind's Tantrums and Luminous Mind's Dance

The next nail with regard to the view is "Mind as such is in the natural state of luminosity." Especially in the Mahāmudrā tradition, the expression "mind as such"[9] refers to the ultimate, true nature of the mind as opposed to the dualistic mind[10] of sentient beings. Thus, this expression is a synonym of the Mahāmudrā hallmark "ordinary mind." It refers to mind's natural state, just as it is on its own, without being messed with in any way. That native mind is the fundamental space of luminosity. As mentioned before, "luminosity" does not mean something like physical light but refers to mind's innate vivid awareness and radiance, as well as its innate purity of all adventitious stains.

Again, for Milarepa, the correct view consists of directly experiencing this spacious and luminous nature of the mind, not just analyzing it in terms of words or concepts. This means that mind's luminosity is inseparable from its basic spaciousness or emptiness. Thus, this luminosity is nothing that can be pinpointed or solidified in any way. Therefore, Milarepa says that within mind's very own natural state, "there is nothing to be identified." In other words, within the fundamental space of mind's luminous nature, there is neither any reference point nor anything to hold on to. As long as we think we have found something that is our mind or its nature, we may have found something else, but it is definitely not the nature of the mind. This is also expressed in some other songs by Milarepa, such as when he sings:

> Throughout the day and night, look at the mind!
> When looking at the mind, nothing is seen
> When nothing is seen, just let go and relax!

When we analyze our mind, we do not find it, but at the same time there is an undeniable quality of experience. This is just as when Milarepa spoke about appearance and emptiness being inseparable earlier. "Appearance" may sound more external, but it applies to the mind just as much as when we speak of experience and emptiness or luminosity and emptiness being inseparable, though they sound more internal. However, on Milarepa's premise that all possible appearances and experiences are nothing other than the mind, the inseparability of appearance and emptiness and the inseparability of luminosity and emptiness are just two sides of the same coin.

There is a commentarial song by Khenpo Tsultrim Gyamtso Rinpoche on *The Three Nails*, called *The Essence of Luminosity's Sunshine*, that explains the nail of "**all possible appearances are contained in the mind**" as follows:

> All possible appearances contained in the mind—what's the
>   point of this nail?
> The appearances of delusion arise from habitual tendencies,
> and all appearances are luminosity's dynamic energy and play
> Thus, they are all contained in the mind—a profound point
>   indeed

Saying that all appearances come from the mind means that both deluded experiences (ignorance, confusion, mental afflictions, and suffering) and undeluded experiences (such as the five buddha wisdoms and nonreferential compassion) are happening nowhere else than in the mind. In particular, the appearances of delusion come from the habitual tendencies of delusion in our mind: the latent tendencies of ignorance, mental afflictions, and so on. These are the mental patterns that produce further delusion and suffering and also reinforce each other.

On the other hand, if mind's true nature is seen, all appearances are realized to be nothing but the dynamic energy and play that is the natural expression of mind's own luminosity. We could say that the dualistic appearances of delusion are the play on the surface of the mind, like waves on a deep and vast ocean. By contrast, the uncontrived, nondual appearances of the nature of the mind are the display of its innate creative dynamics, similar to the totality of water's movement throughout the entire ocean. Still, in both cases, appearances come from, or are nothing other than, the mind. The differences as to what appears and how it appears (solid and claustrophobic or vast, open, and light) lie in whether the true nature of the mind with its natural display is realized or not.

Also, no matter whether appearances arise from the habitual tendencies of delusion or as luminosity's own energy, this does not mean that nothing is going on. To rest in the nature of the mind does not mean to rest in some kind of eternal tranquility or a state of being spaced out in which nothing happens, like a flatline on a heart monitor. Rather, the playful energy and creative display of mind's luminosity is constantly unfolding. Thus, this is the relative and ultimate meaning of the first nail of the view that "all possible appearances are contained in the mind": relatively speaking, appearances arise from mind's habitual tendencies of delusion; ultimately speaking, they arise as the innate play of mind's luminosity.

As for the second nail of the view, Khenpo Rinpoche explains:

> Mind as such is luminosity—this profound nail is hard
>   to realize
> Mind's true mode of being is free of reference points
> and its essence has always been completely pure
> This is luminosity, ineffable—a profound point indeed

Mind is said to be luminosity, but what that actually is cannot be pinpointed. We can give mind's nature the names "luminosity," "buddha nature," "mahāmudrā," "rigpa," or any other name. We can call our mind anything we want—mind does not mind what we call it—but none of these names really gets it, all of them are just pointing fingers. Ideally, the more of these pointers we have, the sooner we get the point. If there is just a single finger pointing to a small star in the night sky, it is not easy to see the star. But if a lot of people point to that star from different directions, it becomes easier.

Milarepa also says that the essence or true nature of the mind has always been completely pure and unstained by anything that goes on within it. No matter how many afflictions we have, no matter how angry or jealous we are, none of that affects the true nature of the mind. Even if there is a hurricane on the surface of the ocean, this does not affect the water several thousands of feet below. Likewise, whatever turmoil happens in our mind, its ultimate nature is not influenced or altered by any of it.

On Milarepa's third nail of the view, Khenpo Rinpoche says:

> As for the nail that this luminosity is unidentifiable,
> it cannot be said that it arises, ceases, or remains
> It's neither being nor nonbeing, nor an object of inference
> Thus, luminosity is unfindable—a profound point indeed

The second nail emphasized that the nature of the mind is not something dead or inert; it is wakeful, vivid, and aware. This third nail says that, despite its vividness and brilliant luminosity, we cannot solidify it even if we try. There is no reference point within the fundamental space of the mind, and its luminosity is in constant motion. That's why the nail here says that it cannot be nailed down, pinpointed, or recognized as anything. Of course, mind's luminosity can be recognized experientially, but it cannot be recognized as a "thing" or a solid entity. We cannot say in any way where a given moment of mind arises from, where it abides, or where it departs to, nor is it possible to find out how it emerges, how it is present, or how it vanishes. Thus, it is not any "being" or any "something." At the same time, since mind's own display is unceasing and appears in all kinds of ways, it is not something like a complete void, an empty vacuum, or a blank state. Therefore, it is not any "nonbeing" or "sheer nothingness." Mind's nature is also not "an object of inference," because it is not accessible or findable through words, thoughts, reasonings, or analysis. When we analyze what the mind really is, we cannot come up with anything. If we come up with something, we have not found the nature of the mind but something else, which is just another reference point, another hang-up.

When these three nails or key points—whatever appears is of the nature of the mind, the nature of the mind is luminous, and this luminosity is empty, spacious, and ultimately unidentifiable—are driven in fully, then that is the view of Mahāmudrā. Again, this is not something theoretical or conceptual but refers to the actual experience of what is taught here.

You may wonder what the hammer that drives these three nails in is. Milarepa answers this at the end of *The Three Nails*:

> Among these nails, a single nail is driven in
> This nail is the nail of empty dharmatā
> The nailing is done by a genuine guru
> If you analyze too much, you won't get it in
> Connate realization is what drives it home

The single nail or key point that includes all nails of view, meditation, conduct, and fruition is "empty dharmatā," which here refers to mind's uncontrived nature, which is luminous, spacious, open, and relaxed. Again, this points to the inner personal experience of what Milarepa teaches here. The "outer hammer" that drives this nail home is a genuine guru who has realized mind's nature and is able to introduce it to us. Based on this introduction, the "inner hammer" is our own "connate realization." This is our mind's innate wisdom itself being aware of its very own nature. This can be understood in two ways: either as realizing "the connate" (the innate nature of our mind that is present within us since beginningless time but unrecognized) or as realizing this nature simultaneously (connately) with the immediate pointing-out instructions of the guru.

We could also say that the nails to be driven in are our mind and the hammer that drives them home is also our mind. More specifically, the nails are the features of mind's nature and the hammer is the viewing or meditating mind. In that way, there is no actual movement of the hammer toward the nails. Or, both the hammer and the nails move toward each other, similar to the famous expression of "mother luminosity" (the ground) and "child luminosity" (the path) meeting, with the child recognizing the mother.

As long as these nails are just words in a book or thoughts in our mind, neither the hammer nor the nails move toward each other; the nails need to be experienced. When the conceptual understanding of what

Milarepa says here becomes our own personal experience, the nails and the hammer move toward each other. Once the hammer of the viewing or meditating mind fully meets the three nails—when mind's spacious luminosity is recognized and the viewing mind completely merges with it—the nails have been driven in. Alternatively, the three nails resemble a mirror and the mind that views them is like the face of a person looking into the mirror: what is seen in the mirror is nothing other than what looks into it.

In Milarepa's *Song to a Pigeon Goddess Girl*, he says,

> ALALA! With this nature of appearance's basic ground
> being introduced as the dharmakāya that is unborn,
> they fuse as the uncontrived dharmakāya's natural state
> Without evaluating whether any view is high or low,
> this uncontrived mind here is so blissful indeed![11]

This presents yet another angle on the view. Again, Milarepa talks about appearances, this time about their essentially being nothing but the dharmakāya, which is the fruitional aspect of the nature of the mind having become fully manifest with all its qualities. When this is pointed out and realized, Milarepa says, appearances do not disappear altogether but their very nature fuses with the natural state of the dharmakāya without any arising, abiding, and ceasing, which is another way of saying that the nature of appearances and the dharmakāya have always been inseparable to begin with. However, it is a matter of whether this is recognized or not. In their very ground, appearances blend right into the uncontrived nature of the mind, because, as Milarepa's *Three Nails* said, they are nothing but an intrinsic part of mind's luminosity and its natural expression or display. The difference between ordinary confused appearances and mind's own natural display manifesting within the expanse of mind's luminous nature is that confused appearances are contrived and fabricated by ignorance and afflictions, whereas mind's innate display is uncontrived, being its own natural radiance, just like the sun and its rays.

Milarepa concludes by saying that he does not care or judge whether his own or any other view is considered to be high or low, because he is talking from within his personal immediate realization of the supreme view, which is free of all views. Anyone who has that experience could not care less about how to describe it or whether it is labeled as a high view or a low view, or any view at all. This accords with how the view is described in the famous Sakya teaching called *Parting from the Four Kinds of Clinging*:

> If there is any clinging, it is not the view

Thus, the "correct" view in terms of experience is a state of mind without any clinging at all, in particular no clinging to any view as being correct, supreme, or better than others.

To compare this to a mundane example, if we are enjoying a piece of wonderfully delicious chocolate, we do not really care about the design of its label, its name, which factory it comes from, its ingredients, or whether it is number one on the chocolate charts. We just eat it and experience it fully in the present moment, without any need to upgrade or manipulate it, without any thoughts about earlier or later. This is the meaning of "Without evaluating whether any view is high or low, this uncontrived mind here is so blissful indeed!" If we just eat our chocolate of mind's unfabricated natural state free of any additives, artificial colors, or preservatives of dualistic perceptions, emotions, or thoughts, and do not think about it (or anything else), we experience all the richness of its full flavor of great bliss. We all know that's true, at least with chocolate, but Milarepa stresses in many of his songs that the experience and realization of mahāmudrā is very blissful.

Last but not least, the third verse in Milarepa's *Anger Cooling Song* says:

> Within the sky of the king of the view of dharma,
> son, train the dexterity of the garuḍa chick of awareness's wings
> Don't let the dexterity of this garuḍa chick's wings get weak!
> Should the dexterity of its wings become weak,
> there is the danger of it falling into the ravine of bias
> Son, Rechungpa, listen to your guru's command![12]

At the time when Milarepa sang this song, his student Rechungpa had one of his anger attacks, because a visiting scholar was insulting Milarepa in debate and Rechungpa felt compelled to end the debate by more forceful means. Thus, Milarepa provided some training in anger management for Rechungpa, telling him, "You gotta cool it, man." That is why this song is called *The Anger Cooling Song*.

Here, Milarepa says that the best view in Buddhism is as spacious as the sky. But it is not like an utterly empty sky, because there is a garuḍa chick within that sky, which symbolizes innate basic awareness. When this awareness is not fully developed—that is, when we just get a taste of the nature of our mind but it is not a stable experience yet—this awareness is like a young garuḍa chick starting to spread its wings and learning to fly. At that point, such awareness is not like a fully grown garuḍa being able to soar through the sky in majestic and completely unimpeded flight. Rather, similar to a fledgling, awareness is just starting to flap its tiny wings. As long as this awareness is in its state of being a baby or even a teenager, we have to be careful not to let its wings go weak on us. The wings of this garuḍa chick of awareness are the luminosity and emptiness of the present moment of basic awareness, working together in perfect harmony in an inseparable manner.

Milarepa says, if we are not careful and let the wings of awareness's luminosity and emptiness remaining in the present moment go weak on us, we plunge down into the abyss of a biased mind. This refers to all the kinds of ego-clinging, rigid views, preconceptions, and black-and-white thinking that make us stray away from the experience of mind's nature without any fixation, fabrication, and discrimination. If basic awareness becomes weak, whatever degree of insight into the nature of the mind that may have been accomplished is lost and we go back to square one, regressing to our deep-seated and all-too-familiar habitual patterns. Our mind literally becomes very narrow (smaller than the tip of a needle), dull, and claustrophobic, and we once again miss out on its vast and spacious openness, brilliant radiance, and crisp wakefulness. Thus, Milarepa warns us of all that by saying, "Son, Rechungpa, listen to your guru's command!"

The main point Milarepa makes in all these songs is that the view he describes is not something conceptual, nor something in a book that we can read, hear, or think about. The view here refers to the initial experience and realization of the nature of the mind. That is what we can actually rely on in following the ensuing paths of meditation and conduct. Even if this experience may not be vividly present all the time, at least we then know through our firsthand experience what it is like. With this experience, meditation is nothing other than the repeated approach of reconnecting with, or rather allowing for, what was experienced as the view to manifest again, as much and as often as possible, but without any expectation that it should happen and without any fear that it won't happen. In that way, meditation is just the stabilization of the initial view, sort of like expanding the trailer of a glimpse of mind's nature into the full movie of the continuous stream of luminosity and emptiness inseparable.

3. Meditation: Awareness in Both Stillness and Movement

Now, let's go back to Milarepa's *Song of Ultimate View, Meditation, Conduct, and Fruition* and discuss its verse on meditation.

> With meditation, this luminosity without grasping,
> there is the danger of getting lost in nothing but resting
> If this wisdom is not dawning from within,
> even if resting is stable, it lacks the dimension of freedom
> Wisdom does not arise within dullness or agitation
> Therefore, undistracted mindfulness is absolutely essential

What does "**luminosity without grasping**" mean? Once we have had an experience of the view, we might try to recreate it in our meditation. Or, if there is an experience of luminosity in our meditation, we may want to keep it, prolong it, make it stronger, and repeat it. All of this is grasping or fixation, which is to be avoided in mahāmudrā meditation. Here, we are not trying to stop anything, but we are not trying to make anything up either, by trying to repeat, contrive, or enhance an experience of the nature of the mind. In fact, such trying is the best way not to experience mind's nature.

Grasping is usually of two kinds: either we try to push something away or we try to get something. These two are otherwise known as hope and fear. In this case they refer to expectations of having a "good" meditation and being afraid of having a "bad" meditation (whatever that may mean). In mahāmudrā meditation, both are to be avoided. We are not trying to have a good meditation, avoid a bad meditation, or eschew bad thoughts or bad feelings. In fact, we are not trying to have any expectations or preconceived ideas about our meditation at all; we are simply relaxing and opening up our mind to allow its true nature to shine forth.

The Mahāmudrā tradition says that whatever appears in our mind, whether in meditation or not, is nothing other than an expression (however distorted) of the nature of our mind. So if we try to suppress or dump all the appearances and experiences in our mind that we don't like, what are we going to work with? How will we recognize the nature of appearances or experiences if we cast them away? Likewise, if we try to keep, manipulate, or enhance those appearances or experiences that we like, how could we recognize their uncontrived nature?

No matter how our mind appears, no matter how grisly its many facets of anger, desire, jealousy, and so forth may seem, these are exactly what we are working with here, whether we like it or not. We don't have a better mind than the one we have. Usually, we think that the nature of the mind is really something much better than our anger. We think it must be calmer, more serene, more peaceful, more nonconceptual, more blissful, or whatever. And then we try to work very hard in our meditation to achieve such a state, which is just another case of grasping and contrivance. We fixate on our fancies about mind's nature and not on our actual experiences. We keep looking for those fanciful images in our mind and we try to create them in our meditation.

We also might try to calm our mind down so that we can have a better look at its nature, because the present thought or feeling feels not good enough or not clear enough to see the nature of the mind. Instead, we are waiting and hoping that the next moment of mind will be better suited for seeing its nature. About calming the mind, Milarepa says here that **"there is the danger of getting lost in nothing but resting."** There is nothing wrong with letting our mind settle and rest, nothing wrong with it becoming calm and peaceful; in fact, this stillness is a necessary prerequisite for directly looking at the still mind through sharp insight. However, such calm abiding alone is not enough. What we need, Milarepa says, is the keen, nonconceptual wisdom that dawns from within.

Technically speaking, in mahāmudrā, when our mind settles within itself, that is called *śamatha* meditation, or calm abiding. But if we leave our mind in just this resting, we miss out on the part of *vipaśyanā,* or superior insight, that cuts through all wrong ideas and clinging and directly sees the ultimate nature of the mind, be it still or moving. This is what **"wisdom dawning from within"** means. It is not enough to simply let the mind rest and enjoy its state of tranquility and peacefulness. Milarepa says, **"even if resting is stable, it lacks the dimension of freedom."** Merely settling the mind, however peaceful, serene, or blissful the experience might be, will not liberate us from saṃsāra or allow us to see the profound nature of the mind.

This is a little bit like floating on an air mattress in a swimming pool on a nice sunny day. We can close our eyes and just hang out there and relax. It is warm, sunny, cozy, and restful. We are not really moving and the water around us is calm too. If we do not move, the air mattress and the water around it do not move either. However, if we want to see our face in the calm water, we will not be able to unless we open our eyes and look into the water. We will not see our face no matter how long we lie still on that air mattress with our eyes closed. Śamatha meditation is like trying not to shake or move that air mattress. But what we really want is to see our mind's own true face in the water of the still mind. Thus, first we need to let mind's stormy waves ebb off, and then we need to look into its calm water. We need to take a good look at our own face, not just hang out with closed eyes and enjoy the sunshine of tranquility and restfulness. Mahāmudrā meditation is not just resting the mind, though this resting is tempting because it feels good. Therefore, Milarepa says in another songs, called *The Prayer of Solemn Commitment*:

> Without clinging to the pool of calm abiding,
> may the flowers of superior insight blossom[13]

Milarepa probably did not have that analogy of the air mattress in mind, but we get the picture. If we cling to our mind's resting and stillness, we may try to make it be without any movement whatsoever. But letting the mind rest in mahāmudrā is not about it being 100 percent or absolutely still. In the analogy of a lake, even if it is very still, its water always has the potential to move at any moment. Also, if we look closely, there are usually a few tiny ripples or currents in its still water. This is similar to our body sitting still in meditation: despite the fact that we are not moving deliberately, our lungs still breathe, our heart beats, and our digestive process is still functioning .

Likewise, our mind always has the natural potential to move; even in its stillness, it may have a few tiny ripples of thoughts here and there. From a Mahāmudrā point of view, that subtle movement is not really a problem, and we don't want or need to suppress mind's natural ability to move. It's more of a problem if we try to keep our mind from having any thoughts or movement at all. What is the most still state of water in a pond that we can imagine? It is a frozen pond—there is no movement at all. However, if the pond is frozen, we cannot see any reflections in its water, nor the fish in it, nor its ground. Also, there is no way for lotus flowers to emerge from it. Thus, this is not the kind of stillness of mind that we are looking for or trying to cultivate in mahāmudrā meditation. In a frozen mind, nothing can be seen, nor can the lotus flowers of vipaśyanā grow in it.

What is the wisdom of vipaśyanā that arises from within? When settled in a state of luminosity free from clinging, letting go completely, our mind takes a look at its own state of calm resting. In Tibetan, it is usually said that we try to see our mind's own face. However, in this case, what looks and what is looked at are the same. How does our mind remain completely calm and look at the same time? It sounds contradictory, because when the mind looks, it moves, but when it just rests, it usually does not look at anything. Especially at the beginning of looking, there is still some sense of moving involved, as well as a slight dualism. It is like the ocean resting still and then one tiny little wave somewhere rising gently and looking at that ocean. This wave is still part of the ocean, not anything different. However, it is as if the ocean puts out a very gentle feeler, so to speak, to look at itself to see what it is. Eventually, that wave also looks at itself, sees what "itself" is and that it also belongs to the ocean it looks at. This is a very subtle and light-handed process.

Thus, when resting in the nature of the mind and then proceeding to look, our mind needs to remain calm as much as possible, taking a subtle peek from within that state. In terms of the vast and still ocean of the mind, this looking is just a slight shift in focus, a tiny little movement.

Our mind looks at its own state of being calm and still. We are not trying to look at the agitated or moving mind at this point. Milarepa says that without the wisdom or awareness that looks at and sees mind's natural face, there is no liberation from our clinging to a self, nor is there any liberation from clinging to the real existence of any other phenomena. Merely through resting, we cannot eradicate the tendency to take things for real, nor can we eliminate the tendency to cling to our hypothetical self.

Milarepa continues by saying, "**Wisdom does not arise within dullness or agitation.**" We may encounter these two problems in meditation, both of which simply mean that our mind is not resting in a mahāmudrā way. When meditating, our mind gets too dull at times; it may feel like resting but it is more like spacing out or falling asleep. Dullness means that the mind lacks its aspect of clarity or wakefulness. Even if our mind is still, it may lack its dimension of lucidity or freshness. There are many different levels of coarse and subtle dullness, from being almost asleep down to some faint sense of haziness or unclear focus.

By contrast, agitation is any state in which the mind moves out of its resting state toward an object, whether this object is outside (the sense objects) or inside (thoughts, feelings, or meditation experiences). In meditation, distractions may be caused by our own experiences, and we may get all excited or worried about that. Often, agitation is a very obvious state of mind not resting, but it may also be subtle, such as thinking, "Oh yeah, that's it!" or "I'm actually resting now." In this regard, the Mahāmudrā tradition speaks of "undercurrent thoughts." Milarepa says that wisdom is not found in any of those states of dullness and agitation.

For that reason, the stability and stillness of calm abiding is a necessary preliminary step for the arising of the wisdom of superior insight from within, because this wisdom cannot emerge from any state of mind that involves dullness or agitation. Thus, Milarepa says, "**Therefore, undistracted mindfulness is absolutely essential.**"

In other words, the basic condition for the arising of the wisdom that sees the essence of our mind is nondistraction, nonwandering, or nondiscursiveness, which is nothing other than mindfulness. It means to be fully in the present moment, without anticipating the future or mulling over the past. In that gap, it is possible to actually look at the present resting mind and see what its true nature is. In order to look, however, we also need to free ourselves from being attached to the state of resting and stillness itself. When our mind is actually resting, that feels nice and we usually do not want to let go of that state. We feel like we finally achieved something in our meditation, so why should we drop that and do something else? It can be quite irritating.

Milarepa says that if we do not have a thought and are just resting, we should look at the resting mind itself, look at that which rests and see what it is. When we have looked at what it is that rests, we also need to look at the looker: What is it that looks at the resting mind? Are the resting mind and that which looks at it two different things or not? Also, if our mind starts moving away from its resting, such as thinking, "I'm resting" or "This is cool," no matter how subtle that or any other thought may be, we need to look right at that thought and see what its essence is. This is the way to work here with inner wisdom in terms of both the still mind and the moving mind. No matter whether our mind is simply just still, whether it looks at its own stillness, or whether it looks at its own movement, to be undistracted and mindful of its sheer stillness, the essence of its stillness, and the essence of its moving, respectively, is essential.

Thoughts Ask, Experience Answers

The way we analyze our mind in mahāmudrā meditation needs to be experiential, not through thoughts, logic, or reasonings. We ask our mind questions, which are, of course, conceptual in some way. But the important point is that the answer must come from our experience, not from yet another concept about our mind. For example, if we ask ourselves what color and shape our mind has, it is not good enough to think, "Of course, mind does not have any color or shape, everybody knows that" and move on. That is not the answer here. The answer can only come from actually looking at our mind when it, for example, sees something blue and rectangular, and then looking at the texture of that experience. We ask ourselves, "Is the mind that sees blue blue? Is it rectangular when it sees something rectangular? What is the difference between the blue and the mind? What is the difference between the rectangular and the mind? What is the difference between the blue and the rectangular in the experience of seeing? Does my mind feel different when I see something red, green, yellow, round, or triangular? If so, how?" All these questions need to be answered based on our own personal experience, not by the standard phrases in meditation books. Also, this kind of investigation is not limited to color and shape but extends to any characteristics that we could describe or find in directly experiencing our mind.

To sum up meditation as presented here by Milarepa, we may have a lot of terms to label meditation, some of them being more experiential and some more technical. But according to Milarepa, meditation is the continuum of mind's own luminosity, free of any clinging, grasping, and solidifying. This is the unaltered nature of our mind, just as it is, without any clouds, obscurations, tampering, or fabricating. If we just manage to simply let our mind *be*, that is a big step toward mahāmudrā meditation; in fact, in mahāmudrā, that could simply be it. If we relax completely, mentally and physically, we are ready or prepared for the highest meditation; or rather, that actually is the highest meditation, in that it is the most natural and uncontrived way of meditating. That is why a lot of teachers explain that meditation is really the deepest form of relaxation.

This aspect of relaxation is primarily the free-of-clinging part of luminosity, but the other important aspect is that meditation here is not *only* relaxation in the sense of just hanging out or spacing out. There are many forms of relaxation, such as going to a spa, watching a movie, or just lying on the couch, but mahāmudrā meditation is different from all those. In addition to the mind being relaxed, there is a sense of vivid awareness and wakefulness, which is called "luminosity" here. These are the two basic characteristics of meditation as described by Milarepa: being completely relaxed but at the same time being wide awake and noticing everything that is going on.

In the two main types of meditation, calm abiding and superior insight, both the aspect of relaxation and the aspect of awareness are present. In calm abiding, we work more with the aspect of mind relaxing and resting, but there still needs to be some awareness. If we lose this dimension, the mind might still be resting, but this resting is not crisp or vivid. In the practice of superior insight, we mainly work with the aspect of awareness. However, our awareness operates within a state of mind still being relaxed and resting. This awareness then focuses on realizing what this mind that is sometimes still and sometimes moving truly is. What is the essence of that which rests? What is the essence of that which relaxes? What is the essence of that which moves? What is the essence of that which is aware?

As Milarepa said, just resting our mind will not lead to awakening or buddhahood. We need this element of keen and sharp awareness, this **"wisdom dawning from within."** The key for that, as Milarepa says, is **"undistracted mindfulness."** Thus, mind's basic state of awareness goes hand in hand with the functional mindfulness on the path. We could say that this basic awareness is like a mother and mindfulness is like her child. This is reflected in the expression of "mother luminosity meeting child luminosity."

Though the functional awareness on the path that we cultivate is called "mindfulness," we need to understand that there are two kinds of mindfulness in mahāmudrā: deliberate or contrived mindfulness and nondeliberate or natural mindfulness. In the beginning, everybody's mindfulness, be it in meditation or otherwise, has some element of deliberation and contrivance, as we make an effort to not be distracted from a given object. But what we actually aim for in mahāmudrā is to reconnect with the most fundamental level of awareness of our mind, which is mind's true condition or its inner space of luminosity, which is naturally aware of its own essence. Eventually, all coarse and subtle ripples of deliberate mindfulness merge back into the ocean of mind's panoramic and nonreferential awareness. Merely not being distracted from that state is what is called "nondeliberate mindfulness" or "uncontrived mindfulness." However, there is no agent that is mindful and there is no referential object to be mindful of. There is no "me" that is mindful, no thought of being mindful, no meditation that is cultivated through being mindful, not even a mind or mental factor that is mindful. Thus, this uncontrived and natural nondual mindfulness is very different from any kind of deliberate or conceptual mindfulness that focuses on an object that is other than itself. Needless to say, this kind of mindfulness is a far cry from the conventional understanding of the term in other Buddhist contexts, let alone what is propagated as "mindfulness" these days in the "mindfulness industry." It simply is the state of being naturally and effortlessly undistracted from mind's essence, without anyone or anything that needs to be mindful.

LIFE IS A DREAM

Let's go through a few other songs of Milarepa to illustrate these points of meditation further. The reason why the view and meditation are emphasized so much in Mahāmudrā is that once we really understand these two, the conduct and the fruition follow naturally and do not need much further explanation. We start by looking at Milarepa's song *Eight Kinds of Mastery*, in which he says the following about meditation:

When dreams and daytime are not different,
this represents the mastery of meditation[14]

When we see our dream life and our waking life as no different, this is the continuous flow of mahāmudrā meditation. That might sound a little funny, but it means neither that we are daydreaming all the time nor that our dreams are the exact same as our waking life. The point here is to realize that both states are illusory. Usually, we think that whatever happens in dreams is illusory and unreal, while what we experience during our time of being awake is real. But as far as Milarepa is concerned, they are exactly the same in merely appearing and yet being empty of any solid existence. It is a good practical exercise to contemplate whether there is any difference between our dream of last night and what we have experienced yesterday in our so-called waking life. From the perspective of today, both are just memories of unique fleeting events that cannot be held on to or replayed. What makes us so convinced that one is more real than the other? From the Buddha's point of view, we are asleep all the time and dreams are just the illusion of dreaming within our more fundamental dream of saṃsāra.

We could also say that the waking state usually is a slightly more stable form of delusion, while dreams are a slightly more unstable type of delusion. Dreams can be very random and we can do all kinds of things in them that we cannot do in our regular world, whereas things in the waking state seem to be more regular—the sun rising every morning, going to work every day with the same car, living with the same people with all their predictable reactions. What is this regularity and where does it come from? It is based on the habitual tendencies in our mind. Those that are more stable—that is, more solid or to which we are more habituated—appear as what we call "the waking state." Those habitual tendencies that are not so stable and can be altered more easily appear as our dream life. From that point of view, the difference is just a matter of degree. Both appearances in dreams and our waking life are expressions of habitual patterns that we have accumulated over different periods of time.

The point is to realize that whatever appears in the mind is like a dream, whether it is in a dream, in the waking state, in our meditation, or during whatever else we may do. Khenpo Rinpoche even says that this life of ours is not really *like* a dream, it *is* a dream. When we think our life is *like* a dream, there are still two things—something that is similar to a dream and the actual dream. But according to the Buddha too, our life *is* a dream. This is why buddhahood is called "awakening": we finally wake up from our endless dream called "saṃsāra" and see that both our waking state (the actual dream) and our dreams (the "double-dream") have been nothing but a single big dream. Once we fully experience and realize that every experience in our mind, no matter what it is, is just a dream, in that it appears yet is empty, we arrive at meditation without sessions and breaks—a continuous stream of luminosity without any trace of grasping or holding on to anything.

Whether we dream or are awake, there are definitely appearances, which Milarepa does not deny. But he says that these are mere illusory appearances, which are not real. Once appearances are completely free of any clinging, delusion, obscuration, and duality, they are nothing but natural expressions of mind's own luminosity. In its pure or natural state, the mind keeps moving and playing all the time. The realization of mind's nature does not mean that nothing is going on anymore. According to people who are in the know about this, there is even more going on, but it is very different. There are still appearances, but there is no clinging whatsoever to these appearances. For bodhisattvas on the bhumis, this is like being in a lucid dream: their experience of dualistic appearances outside of their meditation is like dreaming while knowing that they are dreaming. Therefore, they are not taking anything as real, whereas we take everything so seriously. At the same time, bodhisattvas can still act in that dream of theirs, just as when one becomes good at lucid dreaming, one can change the dream. Thus, bodhisattvas know that everything that happens is a dream, but they still act in a dream-like manner within that dream context for other dream-like sentient beings who do not realize that all this is a dream. As Milarepa says elsewhere:

I regard this life as being like a dream and an illusion
and cultivate compassion for those who don't realize that[15]

In Milarepa's verse on meditation in his *Ultimate View, Meditation, Conduct, and Fruition*, he speaks about luminosity and emphasizes the aspect of not grasping or clinging, which means to realize that whatever manifests from luminosity is not truly existent, just like the appearances in a dream. And when Milarepa speaks of dreams and daytime not being different in his verse on meditation in *Eight Kinds of Mastery*, we again have the two elements of luminosity and not grasping. In our dreams, both the element of appearance and what experiences that appearance manifest from mind's luminosity, and there is also the unreality of both what appears and what experiences it. Thus, we cannot say there is nothing whatsoever in a dream. There is something going on, but we cannot pinpoint it as any solid kind of entity. In principle, the same goes for our waking state. When that is realized in both dreams and the waking state and our mind remains in its present immediate experience but does not cling to it, Milarepa says, "this represents the mastery of meditation."

Beyond Sessions and Breaks

Milarepa's *The Profound Definitive Meaning Sung on a Snowy Range* explains meditation in the following way:

> In the meditation that is the flow of the river of luminosity,
> no sessions of anything to meditate on or breaks can be grasped
> A meditator and what is to be meditated on are undone
>   and gone
> Perseverance in meditation that comes from the heart is
>   excellent[16]

Milarepa speaks again about luminosity, saying that luminosity is like the continuous steady flow of a river, manifesting all the time without any gap or break. Milarepa's own experience of luminosity is an uninterrupted stream, so for him there is no need to make any distinction between "Now I'm meditating" and "Now I'm not meditating." We cannot make any distinction between formal sessions of meditation and the time between those sessions. This lack of any difference between meditating and not meditating nicely matches Milarepa's statement quoted above on the mastery of meditation being represented by the lack of difference between dream and waking life. Once the flow of the river of luminosity is an uninterrupted experience and realization, what is otherwise called "a meditation session" and "not being in a session" are the same.

This also means that there is no duality of subject and object in such a meditation. There is no meditator as something distinct from what is meditated on. In terms of actual mahāmudrā meditation, as was stated above in *The Supplication to the Tagpo Kagyü*, it is even said that we are definitely not doing mahāmudrā meditation if we have a meditation object, no matter what it may be. The whole point here is to step out of the ballpark of duality where we make separations between subject and object, meditator and what is meditated on.

When we say "meditate on" in English, that already implies a duality: there is somebody or something that meditates and something on which that somebody or something meditates. In Tibetan, the word for meditation can be, and often is, used in a sense that does not imply any of that. Especially in mahāmudrā and dzogchen, it is more like meditation is simply happening, without being tied to a self, a meditator, or a doer. It does not involve any agent of meditation or an object, at least not necessarily. As mentioned before, the Tibetan term *gom,* which is commonly translated as "meditation," actually means "to familiarize" or "to cultivate." What is familiarized in mahāmudrā is this continuous flow of the river of luminosity without any clinging, that's all. However, in this process, there is no one who familiarizes and no discrete object to familiarize with.

Milarepa is often said to have declared that "familiarization is not familiarizing; it is to become familiar."[17] That is, in the final picture, familiarization or "meditation" means not to deliberately meditate or focus on anything; instead, it refers to the process of allowing mind's nature to become completely familiar with itself, just as it is, without straying into any kind of unawareness, nonrecognition, or delusion about its own state. Thus, "meditation" in mahāmudrā refers to the process of becoming familiar with what is already there and leaving that be as it is on its own, not making up anything or trying to create or improve anything.

Of course, as beginners, we think that we have to do something in meditation or that we have to follow a technique. This is true at the outset, otherwise meditation becomes kind of random. We might be resting in who knows what. But as we progress on the path of mahāmudrā, there comes a point when the technique itself becomes an obstacle or an obscuration. In the mahāmudrā instructions it is said that, at some point when a certain level of experience in meditation is reached, we need to drop all activities of body, speech, and mind. This means we should not even perform any physical religious activities, such as circumambulating, prostrating, or counting our mala beads, nor should we recite any mantras or prayers. Mentally, we should not entertain any thoughts about what to do or what not to do, good and bad, and so on. All of this is included in the line "a meditator and what is to be meditated on are undone and gone." That, according to Milarepa, is the "perseverance in meditation that comes from the heart," which is the excellent essence of mahāmudrā meditation. If this heart of the nondual and effortless flow of meditation is alive, we do not have to worry about having to sustain our meditation through striving, painful perseverance, deliberate mind-fulness, or thoughts of hope and fear: the continuous stream of the river of luminosity sustains itself on its own in a natural manner.

A Fish Leaping out of the Water

Next, let's look again at Milarepa's *Three Nails*. According to Khenpo Tsultrim Gyamtso Rinpoche's instructions, we also need to contemplate the meaning while we sing songs of realization like these, and then this becomes a singing meditation.

> When the three nails of meditation are explained,
> thoughts are free in their being the dharmakāya,
> lucid awareness is in its natural state of bliss,
> and this is resting evenly without contrivance[18]

We look at these lines through the commentary in Khenpo Tsultrim Gyamtso Rinpoche's song *The Essence of Clear Light Sunshine*. On the line "thoughts are free in their being the dharmakāya," he explains:

> Whatever thoughts may arise, be they good or bad,
> in essence, their arising and ceasing cannot be seen
> Their true nature is stainless luminosity, so he sang
> of the nail "thoughts are free as being dharmakāya"

In the Kagyü tradition, one of the hallmarks of mahāmudrā is that "the nature of thoughts is dharmakāya." This does not mean that thoughts themselves literally *are* the dharmakāya (the term for the nature of the mind in its fruitional state of being free from all obscurations), but the *actual nature* of thoughts is the dharmakāya, which is nothing other than the nature of the mind. If we look directly at a thought and see what it actually is apart from its superficial movement, its conceptual content, and its seeming arising, abiding, and ceasing, the nature of the mind is seen in just the way it is. No matter which thoughts may arise in meditation (or at any other time), whether they are good or bad, in their nature, we cannot find any true arising or ceasing.

When we try to find the moment when our thoughts arise and when they cease, it gets pretty tricky. We can try to find that spot, and that is indeed one of the meditations in mahāmudrā, trying to catch the thought as early on as is possible. Here, the analogy of a fish leaping out of the water is often used—we need to be aware of the thought-fish as soon as the tip of its mouth pops out of the still waters of our mind, not when it is already in midair or when it splashes back into the water. When we look at a lake, we do not know where and when a fish will start to jump out of the water. Therefore, it is very hard to catch that moment. It is also hard to catch the exact moment when that fish disappears again.

Likewise, it is unpredictable as to where and when thoughts arise in the mind. Usually, they arise all the time anyway, so we do not have to worry about having to wait very long for that thought-fish. The problem is rather that there are lots of thought-fishes all the time. Therefore, at least in the beginning, the difficulty is to see one thought clearly within that flurry of thoughts jumping crisscross. When the mind is too busy, it is very difficult to see the arising and ceasing of a single thought. There are too many thoughts in the way, so to speak. We do not see the trees because of the forest. This is the reason why we first cultivate śamatha meditation in order to calm the mind. When there are fewer thoughts arising, there is a better chance of getting a good look at each one of them.

It is almost like being in a lab, where we are better able to isolate things to observe them. If scientists in a lab wish to study a horse, for example, they do not arrange to have a whole herd of horses stampeding through the lab. It is very hard to do any tests on animals that just race by. Rather, they take a single animal and put it in a pen where it is contained and slows down enough to be watched and examined. It is not exactly like that in meditation, because we are not really trying to imprison our thoughts in a cage. But at least we let them slow down, which is the idea of calm abiding. We slow down our speedy mind, which often feels like a bunch of squirrels on crystal meth, and then we have a better chance to look at each one of those squirrels in slow motion to see what they really are made of (if you ever saw the animated movie *Over the Hedge*, you know what I mean).

Thus, we could say that meditation in mahāmudrā means to go from multitasking to "single-tasking" to "zero-tasking": leaving behind our usual busy and distracted states of mind, we look at the essence of a single thought within the state of mind's calm abiding, and that gradually gives way to, or eases itself into, the open and spacious state of simply not being distracted from that very essence in which there is no reference point to focus on.

THE ICE SCULPTURES OF OUR THOUGHTS

Milarepa says that, in essence, the arising and ceasing of thoughts cannot be seen. If we try to find out when a thought arises, where it arises, when it ceases, and where it ceases, we are trying to identify some time and space. However, since we do not find any actual arising and ceasing of thoughts, what are they? Obviously, it is not that nothing happens in our mind at all; many thoughts come up all the time. But Khenpo Rinpoche says that "their true nature is stainless luminosity." We eventually see beyond or behind the superficial appearance of the arising and ceasing of thoughts and see what is actually there. We may compare this to a whole park of well-carved and detailed ice sculptures. When it becomes warmer, they melt away and we do not see their shapes anymore; we see what they really are, which is water. In itself, water does not have any form or shape, but it can take on any form or shape. In the same way, when we look at our thoughts, they seem to have some form, some way of appearing, and some content, but the more we look at them and the more we see what they actually are, they become like water—no particular form or color but very fluid and evanescent.

This also means we see that our mind is less rigid than we thought. When we look at our thinking mind, it often appears very fixed and rigid. We do not even have to have a particular kind of OCD; we can say that saṃsāra itself is one big compulsive obsession. This is more obvious in some people than in others, but if someone thinks their mind is not rigid, they are either lying or they have no idea what is going on in their mind. This compulsiveness of our thinking and the compulsiveness of clinging to what we think is the very nature of saṃsāra. We not only cannot help but be mental busy bees all the time, but we also take everything that we think to be so real and important. Then we create our story lines and they go on and on and on, seeming to become more and more solid all the time, until we arrive at those wonderful ice sculptures that we call our sophisticated and well-thought-out ideas. We completely forget what they are made of and have a hard time letting go of them, despite their being made of nothing substantial at all. Yet we think they are so real, so grave, and so justified, that we hang on to them with teeth and claws, thus getting further and further away from what our thoughts actually are, which is the fluid and playful dance of luminosity without any obstruction or fixation.

This is why Milarepa says, "Thoughts are free in their being dharma-kāya." When we see what thoughts actually are in their very own nature, that is what freedom means: not having a rigid mind, not being uptight, not clinging to anything; every situation is completely open and pliable. This not only means that we are not confused anymore, we are also much more effective in dealing with any situation and any person, because there is no fixed plan. Usually, we think we need a plan A and we also need a plan B and a plan C. One plan is not good enough; we need lots of backup. What Milarepa talks about here is the opposite of that—if we have developed the potential or the capacity to deal with any situation on the spot, we do not need any plan. Life changes all the time and we can never keep up with our plans anyway, as we all know. We make all those plans and then we can see at the end of a week or a month how many of them we actually implemented in the way we expected. We can see that it doesn't happen often. Obviously, the point here is not simply to be completely clueless and unprepared, but to have the internal confidence and power to deal with all situations without preconceptions in an open, spontaneous, compassionate, and skillful way.

We can see this feature in many realized teachers who never seem to have a plan about anything and yet act with amazing sensitivity and accuracy in all kinds of situations. That is also the reason why they always destroy our plans, because they see very clearly that none of them really work. Once, in a dharma center, people were busily preparing for a visit of some rinpoche. Two older Tibetan lamas were sitting there and looking at the people running back and forth trying to organize things and make everything perfect. After having watched this for a while, one said to the other, "It's really funny; they still think saṃsāra works."

This concludes the comments on the first of Milarepa's three nails of meditation, "thoughts are free in being the dharmakāya."

CONCEPT FAILS THE FLAME

The second nail of meditation is "lucid awareness is in its natural state of bliss." Beyond the essence of thoughts being free in their own natural state (the dharmakāya), Khenpo Rinpoche's commentarial song continues:

> Self-arisen awareness, transcending mind,
> in its essential nature is stainless luminosity
> With bliss and emptiness not being different,
> their true reality is something inexpressible
> Awareness, luminosity, and bliss are only distinguished
>   by thoughts—
> in reality, these three are undifferentiable

These are crucial lines. First, Khenpo Rinpoche speaks about "self-arisen awareness, transcending mind." The expression "self-arisen awareness" contains the Tibetan word *rigpa*, used here in the sense of mind's innate, basic state of all-pervasive awareness that does not arise from any causes or conditions extrinsic to it but constantly manifests on its own accord, thus being unconditioned. In that sense, the term *rigpa* is also the hallmark of the Dzogchen tradition, which emphasizes the distinction between this native basic awareness and our ordinary deluded mind (*sem*).[19] Since this fundamental awareness or the nature of the mind is something that is entirely beyond the sphere of our ordinary dualistic mind, Khenpo Rinpoche uses the common Mahāmudrā term "transcending mind,"[20] also used in Dzogchen.

This may sound very far away: "transcending" sounds like somewhere out there or up there. But, as was said before, basic awareness is not far away at all, it is very close, because it is the very nature of our confused mind. The true essence of this confused mind is self-arisen, native awareness. Yet this essence of the dualistic mind is not accessible to the dualistic mind itself, because it is completely beyond the sphere of what the dualistic mind is able to perceive or conceive. Thus, "in its essential nature is stainless luminosity" refers to the nature of that fundamental awareness: it is undefiled by any manifestations of the dualistic mind that may occur within it. At the same time, the experiential flavor of this awareness is not indifference but the great bliss that is without any solidity or grasping; thus, "bliss and emptiness are not different." In reality, when experienced directly, luminous stainless awareness, its feeling of bliss, and its infinite open spaciousness are inseparable and also inexpressible.

When the nature of the mind is experienced and realized, there is nothing we can really say about it that makes any sense, because it is a direct, personal, and unsharable experience. Even in terms of our ordinary experiences, no matter what we say about them, it never really makes any sense; we can never describe any of our experiences in an adequate manner. If someone asks us to describe our experience, we may spend a lot of time talking about it to really convey it. We may go to many therapists, life coaches, or spiritual teachers and spend hundreds of days describing our experiences. Those other persons may eventually get some idea about what our experience might be like, but they can never experience exactly what we do. Instead, sometimes, the more we talk the more difficult it gets to convey anything at all, and on top of that we have to talk even more to clarify others' misunderstandings.

Therefore, Khenpo Rinpoche says, "Awareness, luminosity, and bliss are only distinguished by thoughts." Naturally, the same goes for emptiness. Whatever qualities of the mind we are talking about by isolating them with phrases such as "mind is aware," "mind is empty," "mind is blissful," "mind is clear," all of this is just picking out one element or feature of the entire indivisible experience. To make distinctions is the MO of thinking, not of direct experience or perception. Conceptually, we can talk about the color, the shape, and the heat of a candle flame as being three different things. Conceptually, we are also sure that these are three different things: the color is not the heat, the shape is not the color, and the heat is not the shape either. But when we look directly at the candle flame or put our finger into it, our experience does not separate these three. Experientially, we cannot separate the color, the shape, and the heat as three different things. Likewise, when we talk about the nature of basic awareness, we can use all kinds of isolating terms and thoughts, but they do not describe the actual experience of the nature of the mind. Its three basic features of awareness, luminosity, and bliss (and we can add emptiness as a fourth) are indifferentiable. They represent a single uncompartmentalized experience.

MEDITATION AS UNDOING OUR "DOING-MIND"

Milarepa's third nail of meditation is "resting evenly without contrivance." Khenpo Rinpoche's commentarial song continues:

> As mind's nature is not fabricated or contrived,
> to examine and to contrive are not meditation
> Undistracted, not meditating, without fabrication—
> uncontrived, even resting is meditation supreme

Mind's nature is not something that can be created, contrived, manipulated, or changed in any way. When we try to manipulate our mind or when we try to meditate, we usually think that we are doing something with our mind. In some sense, that is true, but we are never really doing anything with the *nature* of our mind. In fact, we cannot do anything with it, no matter what we do and no matter how much we want to do something with it. The only thing that we can "do" with mind's nature is to get out of its way; that is, leave it alone, let it rest, and let it be what it is on its own. In terms of Mahāmudrā tradition, this is called "returning meditation to its owner": buddha nature or the nature of the mind does a better job meditating than we ever could. We cannot really meditate on the nature of the mind in the sense of this nature being an object and there being a meditator pushing this object around or putting it under a microscope. Ultimately, in Mahāmudrā, we cannot separate the mind that meditates from the mind that is meditated on.

Ordinarily, when we examine things and act, we always think that we need to *do* something. But from the Mahāmudrā point of view, Khenpo Rinpoche says that examining, manipulating, or, in fact, doing anything at all is not really meditation, because it is not in sync with mind's nature being free from all doing and fabricating. Thus, as mentioned before, mahāmudrā is not about doing anything but about undoing or stopping whatever we may be doing or want to be doing.

Of course, in the beginning of mahāmudrā meditation, we need to do some little things, such as cultivating some light-handed mindfulness, focusing, concentration, and so on. But from a more fundamental point of view, those are all just crutches or tools that we cultivate in the beginning to approach something that is beyond those tools and beyond being able to be fixed by them. In other words, we examine and contrive until we finally give up doing so. Any meditation in which we still try to do something is, in some sense, just a tool to tire out our conceptual and clinging mind. When that clinging and conceptual mind finally burns its own fuses or has a heart attack, there is a chance to see what is actually going on. However, since that clinging mind, that watching mind, that "doing-mind" does not leave on its own, we need to work with it by exhausting it.

As paradoxical as it may sound, what we are doing in mahāmudrā meditation is *not* to do anything; what we are working with is *not* to work with anything. This is the hardest thing to do, because one of our most ingrained habits is to always feel we need to do something or we want to do something: we want to fix our car, perform well in our job, improve our life, eliminate our delusion, realize emptiness, achieve enlightenment, have a good meditation, and so on and so forth. From a Mahāmudrā point of view, all of these wantings and doings are simply distractions from, and thus obscurations of, mind's nature just as it is, in which there is no wanting and doing.

Of course, neither Milarepa nor Khenpo Rinpoche say that we should never apply any meditation techniques or that they are all just useless, but there is a progression. First, we need to apply meditation techniques, but we have to be clear on which level they are to be used. They are all used on the level of more or less conceptual and clinging states of mind. Within the realm of the nature of the mind, there is no technique whatsoever, nor can we use any technique. But even in our meditation as ordinary beings, it is important not to get caught up in the techniques and thus forget about recognizing and experiencing mind's nature.

Sometimes our meditation is like wanting to hang a precious painting on a wall in our apartment but then getting stuck on studying all the features of our hammer and our nail in detail—their size, shape, color, design, solidity, weight, and brand names, as well as fantasizing about all the cool things we could do with them—without ever using this hammer to drive that nail into the wall so that we can enjoy looking at the painting.

As Khenpo Rinpoche says here, the key point of mahāmudrā meditation is simply not being distracted from mind's true nature, while at the same time neither meditating on it as being anything nor fabricating it as anything. The main point here is to be one-pointedly focused in a panoramic way without zooming in on anything. This is nonreferential or nondeliberate mindfulness, which sounds like an oxymoron. It just means not being distracted by anything from experiencing mind's very own nature as fully as possible. However, since the nature of the mind cannot be pinpointed, it cannot be focused on it in the same way that we can focus on a book. It is also not a meditation object, such as our breath or an internal visualized image in other forms of meditation,. There is no "thing" there, no reference point, nothing to latch on to. Thus, we are also not trying to create, manipulate, or improve anything here. This approach of not being distracted, not meditating on anything, and not contriving anything is said to be the supreme kind of meditation. Obviously, all of this is discussed very much from an ultimate point of view; it is not a meditation instruction for beginners. That is the reason why Milarepa's song is called *Ultimate View, Meditation, Conduct, and Fruition* and not *View, Meditation, Conduct, and Fruition for Dummies*.

In mahāmudrā meditation, we do not analyze our thoughts or feelings by reasoning or by contemplating emptiness or whatever it may be, we just try to look at the essence of those thoughts or feelings directly. However, "looking" is not meant in a visual sense; rather, we turn the spotlight of our inner prajñā or awareness toward the essence of our thoughts or feelings. Thus, "looking" actually means "penetrating the very core of our experience." This is the mahāmudrā approach: no matter what comes up in the mind or what appears to be an obstacle, we simply turn our awareness right toward that. We do not try to kick out or manipulate anything but just notice it, face it, stay with it, and penetrate to the core of what it actually is.

We could call that "the cockroach approach." If we enter a dark room full of cockroaches, we cannot see them, but we hear them rustling and thus know they are there. Once we turn on the lights, they all zip away. Thoughts are a little bit like that. If we do not shine the flashlight of our prajñā on them, they are hustling and bustling everywhere, but if we illuminate them with the light of the awareness of looking at their essence, they naturally disappear. The seeming solidity of our thoughts and emotions cannot withstand the X-rays of prajñā's gaze of awareness.

When we talk about our own unmediated experience, we need to ultimately have complete confidence in that experience, so that there is no question about whether it is "right" or "wrong." As the scriptures say, once there is unshakeable confidence in our own buddha nature, even if all the buddhas of the three times were to challenge this confidence, it will not waver. Of course, as beginners, it is difficult to first develop and then sustain such confidence. Unshakeable confidence in the nature of our mind does not arise from the very start; it is our innate potential that we rediscover and cultivate.

Unshakeable confidence must be well founded. It does not mean that whatever we think or feel about what we experience is right. When there is true realization, there is not even the thought, "I feel something," "This is right," "I got it!" or anything like that. It is a more organic process of letting our mind take its own natural seat or settle within its very core, which is completely without any ego, bias, or agenda. Since there is no ego, no bias, no agenda, and no reference point in the experience of mind's nature but only overwhelming compassion for others who do not have that experience of their own mind, any action that flows from that experience cannot be wrong, because there is no self-concern. The only striving in such a mind is for the benefit of others all the time, and there is the discerning wisdom of knowing what really helps them.

If we can imagine a state of mind in which we are solely concerned about the happiness of others to the same degree that we are concerned about our own happiness now, that might give us an idea about how much the realization of the nature of the mind is a complete reversal of everything that we do, say, and think. Usually, our thoughts, words, and actions are based on our instinctive tendencies that we are the center of the world and that the world is there to provide happiness for us. However, in a more enlightened state of mind, all we do is based on our wish to provide happiness for the world, without us being at the center. It is simply the compassionate energy of mind in action that is present wherever it is needed in whichever way it is needed.

Dissolving into the Dharmakāya

Now, let's look at the second verse of Milarepa's *Eight Ornaments of the Profound Meaning*:

> Thoughts dissolving within the dharmakāya—
> is that not called self-arising meditation?
> Linking it with experience is great as its ornament[21]

This verse also speaks about thoughts and the dharmakāya. Where do thoughts dissolve? They dissolve into their own nature, which is the dharmakāya. However, thoughts and dharmakāya are not really two different things; the process is more like ice dissolving into water, since the dharmakāya is the very nature of thoughts. When this happens, it is "self-arising meditation" or meditation effortlessly occurring on its own. Milarepa says that this is uncontrived or natural meditation, where we are not holding on to our thoughts or our experiences,

whatever they are, but instead we let them play naturally without trying to stop or improve them, while embracing them with crisp and
undistracted awareness. Then there is a chance that the icebergs of
our thoughts will dissolve into the infinite ocean of the dharmakāya,
which is recognized as being their true nature. When we give our
mind's nature a chance to unfold naturally as it is, as opposed to trying
to force it into something or trying to manipulate it, that is called "self-
arising meditation." We leave our mind as it is, we do not manipulate
it in any way whatsoever, thus letting it do its own thing, but at the
same time we sustain uncontrived nondistraction, which means an
uncontrived awareness of the process of mind expressing itself in its
own natural way as all kinds of things, all of which arise and dissolve
naturally by themselves.

Thus, at least initially, there is an element of watching this process,
but there is no latching on to it in any way. Eventually, there is not
really any difference anymore between the watcher and the process
that is watched. As Milarepa said in *The Profound Definitive Meaning
Sung on a Snowy Range*, "A meditator and what is to be meditated on
are undone and gone." In the beginning there seems to be a meditator
and an object, but then there is just the continuous self-sufficient process of "the flow of the river of luminosity." The expression "to go with
the flow" is of course completely overused, but here it works very well:
meditation is simply going with the flow of the mighty and spacious
river of luminosity-emptiness. It is not even "us" who go with that flow,
because there is no "us" and a flow of luminosity that is different; it is
just that flow flowing on its own, all by itself.

Milarepa continues: "Linking it with experience is great as its orna-
ment." When we go with the flow of the natural play of the mind,
whatever experiences we have, including those in meditation, are its
adornment or dazzling jewelry. If we have meditation experiences of
spaciousness, nonthought, bliss, clarity, or whatever, those are the
"extra bonus materials" that serve as the special adornments of the flow
of luminosity, similar to ever-changing whitecaps on top of the rolling
waves of the ocean. However, none of these experiences ever happens

as long as there is any fixation or clinging, any attempt at manipulating the mind, or any stab at creating or reliving certain experiences.

As mentioned before, the nature of the mind and all the experiences that go together with it are like a gift. We cannot conjure it up, force it, or create it. It is not a product. I guess that is bad news in a society that is product-oriented above all else. The nature of the mind and mahāmudrā meditation are not products in any way whatsoever. They are really worth nothing within saṃsāra, we cannot even sell them on eBay. Whatever we market and sell, it must be something else.

There is a story from India in a commentary on Saraha's "People Dohā"[22] that illustrates this nicely. Once a man had a very crazy elephant. He wished to tame this unruly elephant so that he could employ it for work, but the elephant defeated all his attempts and caused great turmoil, so he became very frustrated and exhausted. Eventually, a friend advised him to sell his elephant so that he would no longer worry and be tired out by his fruitless attempts to tame it. Once the man sold the elephant, his mind was at peace and he recovered from his fatigue. He exclaimed: "This elephant turned my wish for happiness into suffering. Now, having let go of it, I am at ease. If all were to let go of their duties, they would be happy!" His wife heard this and thought to herself: "My mind resembles a crazy elephant: even if I try very hard to tame it, it will not become tame or do what I want. Since I cannot find it as an item that I could sell either, I should just let it go wherever and however it pleases." With that, she remained completely relaxed, not making her mind come, stay, or go. As all her clinging thoughts and emotions dissolved naturally, she realized the great bliss whose nature does not consist of anything whatsoever.

Rest like a Child, the Ocean, a Flame, a Corpse, and a Mountain

Finally, there is another song by Milarepa, called *Six Words That Sum It All Up*, which contains a classic description of how to meditate in mahāmudrā, illustrated through five analogies:

> Do you know the method for letting the mind be?
> If you don't know the method for letting mind be,

without letting mind as such roam around,
don't contrive it with your own mind!

Let it be in its own way, like a small child
Let it be free of waves, like an ocean
Let it be lucid, like a candle flame
Let it be without pride, like a corpse
Let it be immovable, like a mountain
Mind as such has no superimpositions[23]

The five lines that start with "let it be" are the five instructions on how to simply let our mind be in its own natural state, allowing it to rest and settle within itself. As the Beatles say, "Speaking words of wisdom, let it be!" The main point is to let mind rest naturally in its own essence in an uncontrived manner, without clinging to anything or manipulating it in any way. Again, all of this is said from the point of view of mahāmudrā meditation.

First, Milarepa says, "Let it be in its own way, like a small child." This means letting the mind be as open, relaxed, spacious, and thought-free as a small child in wonder. The classic example is a young child entering a Tibetan temple, with its elaborate shrines, colorful brocades, golden statues, copious wall paintings, arrays of offering bowls, multicolored banners hanging from the ceiling, and so forth. When a small child who has never seen such a shrine room enters it, the child is struck by wonder, speechless, and just gazes at all those things, without any thoughts about them. Likewise, Milarepa suggests, we need to let our mind be, just as it is, and simply look at that, without having any concepts or ideas about what we look at or who is looking. We let whatever comes up in our mind (whether it is a perception, a thought, or an emotion) arise and watch it without doing anything with it or entertaining any preconceived ideas about it, such as it being good or bad.

Next, Milarepa says, "Let it be free of waves, like an ocean." This refers to the quality of stillness when resting our mind, like a calm ocean without any waves or agitation. That does not mean that we have to suppress mental movement or thoughts in any way, but that we let the mind rest naturally, with its thoughts and emotions settling on their own, similar to being on the ocean on a day without wind, when the water is still.

Third, "Let it be lucid, like a candle flame." Beyond just resting naturally and still, the mind also needs to be vivid, clear, aware, and wide awake. Especially when we feel dullness, we need to strengthen the luminous clarity of our awareness. In mahāmudrā, awareness is energized through our gaze: we open our eyes more, look out into space, and invigorate our way of looking. While our eyes look at the outside in this way, our mind looks inside at its own nature.

Fourth, "Let it be without pride, like a corpse." This is the best one. It means that if we are dead and have become a corpse, there is no more clinging to a self and no concept of this being "my body." It is just *a* body. Corpses do not have thoughts such as "I'm a good corpse," "I'm a beautiful corpse," "I'm not such a beautiful corpse," or "I'm a fat corpse." In the same way, Milarepa suggests that we should not try to own our meditation, try to own our mind, or think, "I am a good meditator," "I am a bad meditator," "I'm having a nice experience," "I'm having a bad experience," "My meditation is going well," or "It is not going well." All these concepts about meditation are also something that we need to let go of. When they come up, it is not really a problem, but we should not do anything with them. That is what it means to rest like a corpse: not entertaining any self-concerned thoughts or impulses within or about our meditation. As said before, the main question in mahāmudrā meditation is "What is my mind without me?" This is what resting like a corpse means: we just let our mind be what it is, without referring to it as "my mind" or thinking in terms of "my meditation." Resting the mind or letting it be means there is nothing but the mind without "me," just as a corpse is nothing but a body without any "me" or personality. We allow our mind to rest while being free of being puffed up about our practice or our experiences in it.

Fifth, "Let it be immovable, like a mountain." Ideally, the resting mind is unshakeable by distractions, similar to a mountain being immovable by even the strongest storms. This example is somewhat similar to the image of the ocean free of waves. However, the ocean refers more to the mind's natural stillness, while the mountain illustrates mind's being firmly settled or grounded, without any outer or inner conditions being able to disturb that.

These five examples are often used and quoted in teachings on mahā-mudrā. If we can remember them, we basically have everything we need for mahāmudrā meditation. That is, when mind's nature is let be what it is, it is uncontrived, still, lucid, nonconceptual, and without self-concern, as well as immovable by distractions. This also means that there is not really a sequence to these five aspects: they are all elements of a single, undifferentiable experience. They simply describe five features or quali-ties of the resting mind in mahāmudrā. This state of mind is not only still but also clear, thought-free, settled within itself, and without fixation.

However, though these five examples excellently illustrate the way in which the mind is allowed to rest or how it is let be, in the final pic-ture, Milarepa says, "mind as such has no superimpositions." That is, the actual experience of mind's nature cannot be described by any words, thoughts, or examples.

Let Illusion-like Experiences Fly

Milarepa's song *Six Words That Sum It All Up* continues:

> Do you know the way experiences dawn?
> If you don't know the way experiences dawn,
> it's that the sun's dynamic energy dispels darkness
> No need to cast off thoughts somewhere else
> Without any ground, they appear like dreams
> Without any clinging, they appear like water-moons
> Without any substance, they appear like rainbows
> Without any directions, they appear like space

When mind rests as described through the above five examples, what happens? Various experiences will come up. What do we do with these experiences? Essentially, nothing. Just as the sun's energy that mani-fests as light rays effortlessly dispels all outer darkness, the dynamic energy of mind's luminous nature effortlessly outshines the inner darkness of ignorance that manifests as our thoughts, emotions, and dualistic perceptions. With that, we just let them arise and cease in the ways described here, just like illusions or dreams. They manifest, but there is no solidity to them in any way whatsoever, unless we make them solid by hanging on to them and developing our usual story lines.

There is no need to try to cast off our thoughts somewhere outside of our mind, because all of them arise within our mind and naturally cease within our mind, just like waves arising on the ocean and sinking back down into it. Without any solid ground from which they could grow, thoughts arise like the appearances in a dream that equally lack any base and root. If we do not cling to thoughts, they are like a reflection of the moon in water. We clearly see the moon's reflection in water, but we never take it to be the actual moon: it appears vividly as the moon but does not really exist as the moon. Having no substance of their own, thoughts appear like rainbows. Rainbows brilliantly shine in all kinds of colors, but, as we all know, we cannot find the end of the rainbow: it is nothing but light without anything to grasp in terms of a substance. Without any top, bottom, left, right, front, back, or center, thoughts appear just like space, having no size, extent, direction, or dimensionality.

All the examples here, such as dreams, reflections, and rainbows, illustrate the transparent, nonsolid quality of our meditation experiences in mahāmudrā, if we let them just be what they are: fleeting evanescent events in our own mind. We let them arise, change, and cease on their own, just like clouds in the sky form, keep changing their shapes, and eventually dissolve. The fundamental inner space in which our meditation experiences display, as well as these experiences' own nature, are like the vast and open sky without any sides or biases, so there is nothing to identify, pinpoint, or quantify in this space or in the experiences that arise within it.

Milarepa continues:

> Do you know the method for fixing experiences?
> If you don't know the method for fixing experiences,
> though winds may be strong, their natural state is space,
> though waves may be big, their natural state is the ocean,

though southern clouds may be thick, their natural state
  is the sky
Though mind may proliferate, its natural state is unborn

So as to engage in balanced awareness,
see the instructions on consciousness riding the energy
When the thieves of thoughts are showing up,
see the instructions on recognizing these thieves
When the mind strays toward outer objects,
see the instructions on a crow flying up from a ship

Usually, nobody talks about how to fix things in mahāmudrā, because it is said that there is nothing to fix. So here we have the unique chance to see Milarepa describing how to deal with even the strongest and most uncomfortable experiences. It means that whatever turmoil may be happening in our mind in meditation or thereafter, whatever catastrophes, attacks of upsetting emotions, thoughts, and so forth may be occurring, the remedy or way to fix it is not to fix it. Rather, we need to be clearly aware that all of this is happening within the vast space of our mind, just as winds or clouds arise within the sky but can never affect the sky and the biggest waves never affect the depths of the ocean. Whatever thoughts, emotions, or perceptions may arise in the mind, they come out of the mind, play around within the mind, and also disappear within the mind. They do not arise from somewhere else or cease somewhere else.

There is another song by Milarepa, called *Twenty-Seven Cases of Dissolution*,[24] which illustrates the arising and dissolving of whatever appears in the mind through twenty-seven examples. All our thoughts, perceptions, and emotions arise, frolic, and then cease in our mind. So, the way to fix things is to just let our thoughts, perceptions, and emotions do that, not by interfering with them, but by being present with the acute awareness of what their actual nature is. Thus, let them arise, let them do their thing, and let them vanish, but be fully aware of whatever happens and what its true nature is.

The important point is to sustain uncontrived mindfulness throughout this whole process, not just letting our thoughts and emotions run wild. It is not like watching a movie and becoming engrossed in what appears on the screen. Mahāmudrā meditation does not mean being entertained by our internal stories, but to closely watch what is going on, to be fully aware of what is happening in every moment, and to penetrate the very core of that. That kind of awareness is basically the sole "remedy." The remedy is not to manipulate whatever arises in the mind, try to stop it, or try to make it cease quickly, if it is something we do not like. The remedy is watchfulness and undistracted awareness. Milarepa also says here that thoughts may seem strong, but their fundamental nature is unarisen or unborn. In other words, they do not really exist as something tangible in the first place. They may seem very powerful, but other than our own mind just puffing them up, there is really nothing to them. That is why Milarepa recommends we "engage in balanced awareness," which refers to stable but unfabricated mindfulness in the face of whatever may appear.

There is a story about Milarepa sitting in his cave one night when he noticed a thief sneaking in, crawling silently around looking for something to steal. Milarepa listened to him and then burst into laughter. He said, "If I don't find anything to eat in my cave in daylight, how would you find anything at night?" At that, the thief joined him in laughing his head off. Milarepa simply did not possess anything to steal, so the thief's effort was pointless to begin with. In the same way, when we do not engage or follow the thoughts or emotions that come up in our mind during meditation but instead recognize what their nature or core is, there is nothing to steal for them, nothing to gain and nothing to lose. Problems only arise if we follow, become attached to, and solidify our thoughts and emotions. Then there is something to steal, which is the natural state of our basic awareness, free of thoughts and distractions.

Finally, Milarepa says that if we are distracted by something outside or if our mind is all over the place and not focused, we should consider such distractions as being like "a crow flying up from a ship." When we are far out at sea and we let a land-dwelling bird fly from our ship, the bird does not get very far. Eventually, it will always come back to the ship, because the ship is the only place for it to land. In the same way, our thoughts and emotions cannot really go anywhere outside of our mind; eventually, they will always settle back into the very mind from which they arose.

Therefore, we do not have to restrict or nail down our thoughts; it is okay if they move. Even if they move far away, traveling all the way around the world or to other galaxies, we do not have to worry, run after them, or send a search party. Inevitably, they will always settle back where they came from. Nor do we need to reestablish our awareness in a conceptual or contrived manner. We just come back to the present moment of awareness; that's it. If we become distracted, we do not need to follow up on the distraction, such as investigating, "Why was I distracted? What was this about? How do I get back?" We simply come back to the present moment of awareness without further pursuing anything else.

These three stanzas in Milarepa's *Six Words That Sum It All Up* seem very beneficial for mahāmudrā meditation, so to look at them more than once is probably a good idea.

4. Conduct: Beyond Dos and Don'ts

NEXT, WE COME to the section on conduct in Milarepa's *Ultimate View, Meditation, Conduct, and Fruition.*

> **With the conduct, a continual flow free of attachment,**
> **there is the danger of getting lost in nothing but foolish jokes**
> **If the view and meditation do not show up as its companions,**
> **the conduct of yogic discipline and the eight dharmas**
> **become friends**
> **Therefore, to be free of clinging and obscurations is**
> **absolutely essential**

Milarepa says that conduct is "**a continual flow free of attachment.**" The conduct that Milarepa talks about here is natural conduct without any dos and don'ts or any vows to keep. It is the natural behavioral outflow of someone like Milarepa being able to remain in the nature of the mind while being active. This is the continual flow of conduct that is without any attachment to good actions and any aversion to bad actions, whether other people like those actions or not, and whether those actions are beneficial to oneself or not.

However, with this kind of conduct, "there is the danger of getting lost in nothing but foolish jokes." In his comments on this verse, Khenpo Rinpoche says that a lot of people talk about high conduct, especially in the Tibetan Vajrayāna Buddhist tradition. Often, he says, these are just words and vain actions without the underlying realization or true experience of mind's nature. The famous Nyingma master Longchenpa similarly declares that some people think advanced conduct is to dance around naked in public, maybe even in the middle of a large crowd. But, he says, such things will only be the cause of creating distrust in people.

Crazy Wisdom

Of course, we have heard all those stories of crazy yogīs and yogīnīs, crazy wisdom, and so forth. However, when His Holiness the Dalai Lama was asked once about crazy wisdom, he said, "I do not really know anybody who has crazy wisdom. There are a few guys up the hill in Dharamsala who have been meditating there for a long time in retreat. Maybe one or the other of them has crazy wisdom, but otherwise I don't think so. There is an easy test: just offer someone who supposedly has crazy wisdom a really delicious meal and then offer them a plate full of shit. If they delight in eating the one as much as the other, maybe there is some crazy wisdom. Otherwise, forget it." Another comment on crazy wisdom is that many people are pretty good with the crazy part, but seem to still be working on the wisdom part . . .

This is what Padmasambhava has to say on the relationship between the view and conduct:

> Our view is as high as the sky,
> but our conduct is as fine as barley flour

This means that those who have the highest view, which is very vast and spacious, pay even more attention to every detail of their actions. They are completely aware of everything that they do, as well as the beneficial or harmful ramifications it may have for other people, even in the long term. Thus, having a high view does not necessarily mean to do crazy things—more often than not, it does not mean that at all. There are only very few people who are able to demonstrate their realization in ways that may appear strange or impressive but at the same time carry tremendous benefit to others; such people do not simply act crazy for no good reason, such as just having fun or showing off.

For example, the famous—or notorious, depending on whom you ask—Tibetan master Drugpa Künlé (1455–1529) did a lot of things that from a conventional point of view were extremely weird, if not outrageous. But every time he did something like that, it served as a profound teaching for someone. He did not just do crazy things that left people wondering what that was all about or caused them to lose faith in the dharma; there was always some element that blew people's minds and cracked their fixed concepts.

One day, Drugpa Künlé met a man on the road who had heard about this great master and recognized him. The man was carrying a precious scroll painting, hoping to have it blessed by the famous abbot of a nearby monastery and planning to ask him to add in the golden contour lines of the depicted deity. But since he met Drugpa Künlé, he requested, "Since you are the great master Drugpa Künlé, please bless my painting." In answer, Drugpa Künlé spread out the painting in the middle of the dusty road (which is already very disrespectful in a traditional Buddhist environment) and then urinated on it. Of course, the man was not amused, to say the least. He started to shout at Drugpa Künlé, who just walked away. The man was desperate about his ruined painting but rolled it up and proceeded to that monastery. He told the abbot there about what had happened and asked him to check whether he could still save the painting. When the abbot unrolled the painting, he said, "Look, your painting has already been blessed!" The man saw that all the contour lines of the deity were perfectly in place, as if having been gilded with masterful fine brush strokes. Thus, what Drugpa Künlé did was obviously not just peeing on a painting. If someone can do such things, their conduct is fine. For all others, it is not recommended to pee on scroll paintings or other things; in the US, one can get arrested for that.

That is why Milarepa says that this kind of conduct is in "**danger of getting lost in nothing but foolish jokes.**" Some people may pretend they have "advanced" conduct or feel licensed to act not according to the standards of other people, but the main point is always whether they also are immersed in the ultimate view and meditation. If there is no stable basis in our mind in terms of the realization of mind's nature, any such conduct on the outside is just a pretentious hoax. More important, as in the above example, if someone with realization displays unusual forms of behavior, there is usually some beneficial effect for other people. But that can only happen if there is a certain degree of realization, because only then is there no self-concern and ego-clinging, or at least not much, on the side of the one who displays such conduct. Also, there is enough openness in someone like that to see what is actually going on in other people and what is helpful for them. Obviously, the point is not to show off whatever we think we have realized or our imaginary transcendence of ordinary standards of social conduct; that is not crazy wisdom or what conduct means here.

Therefore, Milarepa continues, "**If the view and meditation do not show up as its companions, the conduct of yogic discipline and the eight dharmas become friends.**" If we lack the ultimate view and meditation, whatever we may perceive as advanced conduct just becomes an expression of being caught in the eight worldly dharmas: being attached to and trying to achieve our own gain, praise, fame, and happiness, while trying to avoid and eliminate any kind of loss, blame, disgrace, and suffering at all costs, even if these actions are to the disadvantage of others. If, as Buddhists, we act on the basis of these eight, be it consciously or unconsciously, we are not only back to square one, but our actions are even worse. For we fool ourselves by thinking that we behave in a really advanced or good way, whereas all we accomplish is to reinforce our usual negative habitual patterns by acting out of egocentric considerations about what we can gain or lose, how we can preserve or improve our reputation, gain more accolades and credits, increase our physical and mental comfort, and push the burdens of dishonor, being at fault, and misery onto others. In that way, our conduct is not only far from being beneficial to others, it most likely puts them off or even harms them.

"**Therefore, to be free of clinging and obscurations is absolutely essential.**" In other words, and this runs like a red thread through Milarepa's entire song, if there is any clinging, no matter to what it is, we are in trouble. As mentioned before, if we have any clinging, we do not really have the view ("**the wisdom of being empty**"). If we have any clinging, it is not meditation ("**luminosity without fixation**"). If we have any clinging, it is not conduct either ("**a continual flow free of attachment**"). So forget about any kind of fruition that is worth the name.

However, often when we speak about conduct, there is a lot of clinging involved. Even within the Buddhist tradition, there is a lot of clinging. We have all kinds of different vows on many levels. First, there are the refuge vows, and they include some small print in terms of what we are supposed to do and not do afterward. Then, there are the prātimokṣa vows. Among them, we can take a number of lay vows or all five. Or we can even decide to become a monastic and then may have many dozens of vows to keep, all the way up to 365 vows for fully ordained nuns. Next, there are the bodhisattva vows, with a substantial number of main and secondary precepts. Finally, we have the Vajrayāna vows, which are even more in number.

Thus, even within Buddhism, it just seems to get worse and worse as far as sticking to the rules goes. We may wonder where there is any freedom from clinging in all of that. In general, all those vows are intended to be aids until we are truly free from clinging, because as long as we are not, it is still better to cling to what is conducive to eventually lead us to this freedom from clinging. This is a gradual process and it is hard to jump from full-fledged clinging right into a total lack of clinging. All those vows, rules, regulations, and dos and don'ts were developed in order to facilitate that process of gradually moving from tenacious clinging to being free of all clinging; they were not designed as something new to cling to as the ultimate truth.

We may take some vows and then become obsessed with having to keep them, how to keep them, what exactly an infraction is, what breaks these vows, how we can restore them, whether others keep their vows, whether they need to be punished or expelled if they don't, and so on. We may deem ourselves pure practitioners and keepers of our vows, while looking down on people who do not have them or those who we think do not keep them as perfectly as we do. All of that is just further clinging and not the kind of conduct that Milarepa talks about here: the vast and spontaneous actions of body, speech, and mind that are the natural outflow of profound realization.

What does freedom from clinging mean? Here, Milarepa says that clinging manifests as being attached to the eight worldly dharmas, which show our habitual patterns for ordinary ways of behavior, all of which are grounded in clinging to our self. Our usual ways of conduct are all based on doing what seems good or pleasurable for us and fending off what seems bad or unpleasurable. The thrust of our conduct is clearly in that direction, but the conduct that Milarepa talks about is headed in the exact opposite way. In this conduct, we are not looking at what is good for us but at what is good for others. Ideally, in the ultimate conduct that Milarepa discusses here, we are not even thinking about what is good for others—our conduct is simply the spontaneous altruistic expression of our realization, which means being naturally kind, compassionate, and helpful to others in any skillful way possible. We can see such conduct in a number of great beings on this planet, who perform it in an effortless and consistent manner, such as Mother Theresa, the Dalai Lama, Saint Francis, Mahatma Gandhi, and others like them.

Thus, the view, meditation, and conduct of Mahāmudrā do not mean that we forget about compassion and everybody else. This path is not some kind of navel-gazing of only being concerned about our own precious mind; rather, what we do when we interact with others and how we do it depends on the level of our capability of practicing with our mind. Milarepa talks about view, meditation, and conduct from the point of view that, when we actually realize what is described here, our conduct is perfect in terms of what is right and wrong, because it operates naturally from within a deep inner realization of how things truly are. At that point, we do not need any rules about what is right or wrong; we do not even have to think about such things. Instead, we spontaneously do the right thing in each situation, because we have a tremendous amount of space to see both our own mind and everybody else's mind too, as well as great compassion for those who do not see in this way. Thus, compassion is a package deal and is included in the realization of mind's nature. Milarepa does not explicitly mention this here, but there is no realization of mahāmudrā without profound compassion, otherwise it is something else. It is often said that if we do not cultivate compassion and practice the path of a bodhisattva (such as the six pāramitās), it is impossible to realize emptiness or mahāmudrā. It simply does not work.

Naturally, when we are beginners on the path, our meditation and conduct are at a different level. We try to cultivate compassion, we do *tonglen*, and we try to train in the bodhisattva path by helping other beings in our more or less limited ways. All of this is very necessary, and in others of his songs, Milarepa discusses compassion when he speaks about conduct on the level of relative reality. But here he only speaks about the ultimate kind of meditation and conduct: the experience or realization of mind's nature and the spontaneous actions that result from that.

When we sit on our cushion doing formal meditation, we do not engage in other things. As long as we have meditation sessions and periods where we do not meditate, there is a distinction between our meditation and our conduct. The main point here is that if we work with the kind of meditation that Milarepa describes, due to the freedom that we gain in our mind through that, our conduct will automatically improve. In addition, such meditation and conduct enhance each other. The point is obviously not to have all kinds of wonderful supramundane experiences and qualities in our meditation and then revert to our regular trips as soon as we leave our cushion. In our practice as a whole, our conduct is meant to enhance our meditation, and our meditation is designed to enhance our conduct. That is why a number of teachers recommend alternating meditation retreats with going back into the regular world to see how our minds behave in the context of interacting with the situations of ordinary life.

IF WE LET IT BE, MIND NEEDS NO FIX

Milarepa's *Three Nails* discusses conduct in the following verse:

> When the three nails of conduct are explained,
> the ten virtues arise as the natural expression of conduct,
> the ten wrongdoings are naturally pure in their place,
> and being lucid and empty can't be contrived by a remedy[25]

Khenpo Rinpoche's commentarial song on the second line says:

> When mind's nature is realized as luminosity,
> all movements of body, speech, and mind are pure
> The genuinely true virtue has been manifested,
> so the ten virtues represent natural conduct

Thus, when mind's nature is realized, whatever we do with our body, speech, and mind is naturally pure and naturally virtuous. Here, "virtuous" does not mean being a good boy or good girl by following the rules. It means to do what is best for others in every moment and to do it in a way that is as natural as we presently strive to do good things for ourselves. Outwardly, such conduct usually appears as the ten virtuous actions (such as protecting life, speaking the truth, and benefiting others).

What happens to negative deeds then? Khenpo Rinpoche explains Milarepa's third line as follows:

> When it is realized that mind does not really arise,
> all evil thoughts are pure in their very own seat
> The one committing wrongdoing is always pure too,
> so the ten wrongdoings are naturally pure in their place

Of course, at the level of conduct described here, one does not really perform any negative deeds anyway, but there may still be some nasty thoughts coming up. However, when it is realized that mind does not really arise, all negative or nonvirtuous thoughts are pure right in themselves. Even if they come up, they are realized right away for what they are—unborn, unreal figments of imagination, just bubbles in the mind—and then there is no need to pursue any of them. They just pop up and then they pop down, and that's it. There is no reaction to them and thus no ensuing conduct based on them. Likewise, the one who has a negative thought and then might act it out is also just a bubble in the mind, so there is no need to solidify or pursue that either.

Therefore, "the ten wrongdoings are naturally pure in their place." If it is realized that negative thoughts, which would otherwise cause negative actions, arise from the mind, and they are not followed or solidified, they naturally dissolve back into the mind from where they arose; this is all that happens. There is nothing negative about that, nor is there anything positive about it either. It is just the mind's play happening in the mind. Any negative or positive twists to this play only happen if we solidify or cling to the thought, think we have to do something about it, and act out in one way or another because we feel we are right or entitled, or whatever our reason may be.

Finally, Khenpo Rinpoche comments on Milarepa's fourth line:

The remedy, the prajñā of realizing selflessness,
does not contrive lucid and empty mind at all
and the remedy itself is naturally pure and free,
so it cannot contrive being lucid and empty

This is the very foundation of conduct. The fundamental remedy for ignorance and all obscurations is the wisdom of realizing that there is no self and no truly existent phenomena either. However, this wisdom does not make the nature of the mind any better. In other words, if the nature of the mind is realized, that does not improve or upgrade this nature in any way, just as the sun is not improved when clouds lift, nor damaged when it is covered by thick clouds. It is only those below the clouds who might think that the sun has deteriorated or disappeared. Remedial wisdom is naturally pure and free in itself; it is not something solid to hang on to or to solidify in any way. The only way in which this wisdom "removes" all delusion and obscuration is through clearly realizing that what appears as delusion and obscuration did not really exist in the first place. However, this wisdom does not create, contrive, fix, or improve mind's nature, which is perfect in itself in being luminous and empty by nature, nor does it produce buddhahood.

Therefore, the conduct on this level arises naturally and spontaneously from the realization of mind's luminous and empty awareness. The conduct that is the natural expression or radiance of that realization is not something that we can plan or strategize, no matter how hard we try. There is no way we can ever successfully pretend to engage in this kind of natural conduct if we do not possess the underlying realization, no matter how inventive we may be. Sooner rather than later, we will trip up. If we have had enough contact with realized masters, this point will be obvious. They have no thought-out strategies or long-term plans in our sense, and usually not even short-term plans. Our problem is that we have a lot of plans and strategies, but eventually they all get busted.

From the ultimate point of view of Mahāmudrā, there is really nothing to do in terms of conduct. We are not doing anything, but we are done in a double sense: the conduct does us, and at the same time our ego is done. There is no self-involvement in this conduct: our self is gone, and any action that happens out of the realization of mahāmudrā is not done by "us" but by the nature of our mind, which is a completely different MO altogether. It is the ultimate upgrade of altruistic conduct.

When we say that there is nothing to do, it sounds like realized masters don't do anything anymore at all. But if we watch them, we see that they constantly do a lot, and they even do it much better—more effectively, for many more beings, and with a lot more compassion, clarity, and insight—than we do. All those qualities that we usually want to have as bodhisattvas, such as getting our actions right, getting them done in time, and being of great benefit to others, do not really manifest as long as we have our ego-based agendas and strategies. Such qualities may arise to some extent, but we do not yet fully tap into the infinite potential of our mind, which is what naturally manifests all those qualities in our actions.

Usually, we think we need a plan or a strategy, otherwise we cannot really do anything meaningfully. We cannot imagine how it would be to act without any sense of self. However, even in our ordinary life, there are situations where we actually do act in such a way without realizing it, and usually these are very enjoyable situations.

For example, when we begin to learn how to play a musical instrument, we are very clumsy and conceptual about it. We have to keep many things in mind, such as how to hold and move our fingers, look at the notation, and so on. In addition, our teacher interferes with our efforts, telling us we are not doing it right. But once we learn to play really well, it is basically not "us" playing but just a seamless process of mind, hands, instrument, and sounds interacting, a natural and pleasant flow without any ego or self-concern. We *are* the music. We do not think any more about the left hand and the right hand, where to put the fingers, and so on. In fact, if we think about these things or if we become self-conscious, this spontaneous flow becomes interrupted. Obviously, there are many more examples like that. In brief, if our body, speech, and mind are completely immersed in something, as the nice English expression "losing ourselves in something" indicates, there is actually no conscious experience of ego for the time being, which is usually very delightful.

We may sometimes wonder what it would be like to be without a self or ego. Most people think it must be boring, that we would lose our cherished and vibrant personality, and that we would become some kind of zombie. But actually, as the above example illustrates, being without ego is the most pleasant and inspiring state of mind to be in. Buddhism always talks about the supreme realization of "no self" but not so much about what that experience or realization feels like. Maybe that is why most people don't believe it is worthwhile, so probably the marketing for selflessness needs to improve.

5. Fruition: Nothing to Gain, Nothing to Lose

FINALLY, Milarepa sings about the ultimate fruition:

> With the fruition, this nakedness that is bare of any stain,
> there is the danger of being dressed up in characteristics'
> costumes
> If this delusion does not fall apart from within,
> you may meditate with wishful thinking but have little idea
> about the real point
> Therefore, it is absolutely essential for delusion to fall apart

What does "**nakedness**" mean here? In the beginning, we talked about the ultimate view: "**the wisdom of being empty**" or the nature of the mind, just as it is, which is also known as buddha nature. The fruition is nothing other than this very nature of the mind. "Naked" means that it is finally free from all the adventitious stains that seemed to obscure it. It is not dressed up or shrouded in any garments of extrinsic stains, crazy emotions, or weird thoughts. It is the self-arising wisdom that is aware of its own nature and free from the entire cocoon of fleeting obscurations. If we are naked, that is how we actually are by nature; it is how we came into this world. Afterward, we put on all these embellishments, such as clothes, shoes, hats, jewelry, makeup; we keep adding layer after layer to cover our nakedness. In the same way, in ordinary beings, the nature of the mind is dressed up in all kinds of obscurations, which are what is called saṃsāra.

From this point of view, it seems saṃsāra is some kind of mental Halloween, with lots of different costumes. We run around in all our fancy attire and think of ourselves as being cool, because we have the best outfit—so original, inventive, fashionable, special, and sophisticated, and definitely so unlike the stupid, cheap, or primitive costumes of others. However, from the point of view of the nature of the mind, no matter with what guise we may dress up our mind—be it a powerful god, a rich business person, a Hollywood star, a cute animal, a frightening monster, or the devil—all of that is just a charade. Thus, saṃsāra is an eternal Halloween party, but there are only tricks and never any treat.

Next, Milarepa says that this ultimate fruition is in "danger of being dressed up in characteristics' costumes." It risks getting talked to death by being labeled with all kinds of lofty names and attributes. We can call it "the nature of the mind," "buddha nature," "ordinary mind," "luminosity," "mahāmudrā," "dzogchen," or whatever we want. The nature of the mind does not really mind what we call it. But talking about it and conceptualizing it is not the fruition or realization. In the process of trying to strip mind's nature of all its ordinary saṃsāric clothes on the Buddhist path, we might end up dressing it up in even fancier Buddhist conceptual costumes. These might look better from one point of view, especially if we are a Buddhist, but they probably look even weirder from the point of view of others. In any case, from the perspective of mind's nature, Buddhist costumes of characteristics are no better than any others. It makes no difference whether we are fettered in prison by an iron chain or a gold chain. We may get excited about our wonderful golden chain, marvel over its beauty, and praise it in the most eloquent ways, but we are still chained up and in prison.

THE HOSE AND THE SNAKE

Therefore, Milarepa continues, **"If delusion does not fall apart from within, you may meditate with wishful thinking but have little idea about the real point."** What does it mean for delusion to fall apart from within? It is different from our usual concept of overcoming something: we may think we need to grab delusion and knock it out, putting it in a sturdy box and sending it far away to dump it in some safe place forever. But letting our delusion fall apart, collapse, or simply fade away on its own is not at all an aggressive act; it is not even something that is actively done. According to Khenpo Rinpoche, it means that all appearances of delusion sink back into, or settle naturally within, the expanse of the luminosity of self-arising wisdom. This is the principle of letting our delusion settle (similar to dust settling) and thus vanish on its own. In other words, this means to realize delusion's true nature of being nothing but a fleeting illusory appearance without any real existence of its own in the first place.

For example, when we mistake a hose with a zigzag pattern for a snake, apart from our imagination, there is no snake at all. Therefore, we do not have to kill or physically remove the "snake" in order to see the hose, we only need to take a close look and see that this "snake" does not exist. Once we are completely certain about this, we will not repeat the mistake of confusing that hose for a snake. Likewise, the realization that the dark clouds of our delusion are illusory and that all there is is nothing but the luminous space of mind's nature can only happen from the inside, by taking a close look at the nature of our delusion, seeing it for what it is (not truly existent), and recognizing what is actually there (mind's open, spacious, and luminous awareness).

Otherwise, Milarepa says, we are fooling ourselves in that we "**may meditate with wishful thinking but have little idea about the real point.**" In other words, we may aim very high in our meditation, but there is not much benefit or power to it. We may think, "Wow, now I'm doing mahāmudrā meditation, that's so cool!" or "I'm working with the mind of clear light." We may feel really good about this until we realize it does not work for us. Then we look for the next practice that sounds exciting, such as dzogchen or some exotic deity visualization, trying that one with the same attitude until we find it does not work either, and so on. What Milarepa means here is that we may get hooked on some ideas about what mahāmudrā or dzogchen is, how great it is, and how we can realize it. Then, in our meditation, we try to conjure up something that seems to correspond to our ideas about dzogchen, mahāmudrā, or the latest fad in the spiritual supermarket.

Needless to say, such an approach is entirely conceptual and contrived; it is not really meditation from the mahāmudrā point of view. We basically just try to confirm and sanctify our own ideas. Or, even if we had some genuine experiences, subsequently, we may keep chasing after them, dwell in recollecting them, or try to reproduce them. If we get stuck on our own ideas about certain kinds of meditation or what experiences and realization are about, our practice might not be completely pointless and there might even be some small benefit in it, but it is definitely not cutting to the chase as far as mahāmudrā is concerned.

This is why Milarepa concludes that "**it is absolutely essential for delusion to fall apart.**" Throughout the path, from the starting point of working with the view all the way up to the fruition, we always need to watch out for fooling ourselves and for dressing up what we think we have achieved in embellishing words, concepts, and emotions. "Delusion falling apart" refers to all our inner delusions in terms of view, meditation, conduct, and the fruition. We need to check whether what we do on the path is still for real or whether we have strayed into something completely different that we fabricated on or own. Of course, this is sometimes hard to figure out without an experienced teacher as a guide, because it is the specialty of our ego to claim everything, even the path that is supposed to see through ego's tricks and its fundamental nonexistence, as its own territory and embellishment.

This is also one of the reasons why it is said in the Mahāmudrā, Dzogchen, and Vajrayāna traditions that we should not talk too much about our experiences in meditation, or at least not to everybody all the time. When we put our meditation experiences into words, we conceptualize and generalize direct unique experiences, which actually leads us further and further away from these immediate experiences themselves and makes us get stuck on the nice concepts that we created *about* our experiences. Every time we tell someone the story of our special meditation experiences, it just keeps getting better and better and more and more embellished. In the end, all we deal with are the concepts about our experience, which are far removed from the actual, original experience and thus prevent us from having further genuine experiences and realizations. This is considered a serious obstacle, because we are not looking at the full moon of our experience anymore but just at more and more fingers that seem to point to it, whereas they actually lead us away from it.

NOTHING TO BE REMOVED OR TO BE ADDED

To discuss the fruition in a bit more detail, we look at Milarepa's *Three Nails*:

> When the three nails of the fruition are explained,
> nirvāṇa cannot be brought in from somewhere else
> and saṃsāra cannot be cast away somewhere else
> I've made up my mind: my own mind is the buddha[26]

Khenpo Rinpoche's commentarial song explains the second line as follows:

> The ground is luminosity, the very tathāgata heart
> Nirvāṇa is its true reality, its natural way of being
> The three kāyas are present all by themselves,
> so nirvāṇa cannot be brought in from somewhere else

Nirvāṇa or the three kāyas (that is, the full and final dimensionality of the realization of mind's nature) is not something that is created somewhere outside of this nature and then imported from there. These days, almost everything is imported from somewhere, but this fruition is not brought in from anywhere. It is nowhere to be found other than within our own mind. When we talk about things like nirvāṇa, the three kāyas, or buddhahood, they often sound very distant or highfalutin. We think of nirvāṇa or buddhahood as the state when we finally "get it," in which we can hear the heavenly trumpets playing while the angels or the ḍākinīs sing our praise.

All of this is again nothing but conceptually dressing up the realization that these terms refer to. From the mahāmudrā point of view, even all the Buddhist teachings about the ultimate fruition—such as the three kāyas, the nonabiding nirvāṇa, the five wisdoms, pure buddha realms, and so on—are just more layers of dressing up the nakedness of the immediacy of direct realization. Maybe they are somewhat nicer outfits, at least for Buddhists, but they still veil the natural state. As long as the realization that those words and concepts point to does not dawn within our own mind, it is definitely not the ultimate fruition. The verse here also points out that the ground—the luminosity of buddha nature—is nothing other than the fruition that is called the nirvāṇa of buddhahood; buddhahood is simply the natural state of buddha nature once it has become free from all its adventitious illusory stains. In other words, the fruition, also known as the three kāyas, is already present at the time of the ground in all sentient beings in an obscured manner as the nature of their minds. Therefore, there is no new or different fruition to be brought in from anywhere else.

On the third line of Milarepa's verse, Khenpo Rinpoche explains:

> Saṃsāra is just the movement of thinking mind,
> saṃsāra lacks a root and is without any base,
> and those circling in saṃsāra never existed,
> so saṃsāra cannot be cast away somewhere else

From this point of view, saṃsāra is just the creative movement of our own mind projecting all kinds of illusory appearances. In other words, our own saṃsāra consists of nothing but our own thoughts, perceptions, emotions, and projections. Saṃsāra is not even a big or long thing, though Buddhists usually talk about saṃsāra as being beginningless and endless. But where is that long saṃsāra without any beginning and end? In terms of our immediate experience, saṃsāra is always just one moment, which is the present moment. Our personal experience of saṃsāra is nothing but a single moment at any given time. That is also the beginning of our own saṃsāra in each moment, rebooted again and again.

Realizing saṃsāra as what it actually is is similar to realizing that the hose that we mistook for a snake has never been a snake and that this "snake" existed nowhere else than in our own mistaken perception. It is nothing but this realization that is the end of saṃsāra and the simultaneous beginning of nirvāṇa. Saṃsāra is without any solid ground, basis, or core whatsoever: it is nothing but the appearances of delusion, like a dream. Those who circle in saṃsāra, or rather those who dream they are in saṃsāra, have never really existed either. Both the beings in saṃsāra (the experiencers of the dream appearances of saṃsāra) and the objects that they experience are equally illusion-like and dream-like. Therefore, since neither saṃsāra nor those who experience it truly exist as any solid entities or beings, even if we want and try to cast them away somewhere else or deport them to some dumping ground, we are unable to do so, because there is nothing to throw out or banish in the first place. How can we deport a dream? We are not even able to transfer it into our own waking state, so where would we be able to send it? Certainly nowhere outside of our mind.

In other words, the strategy to attain the fruition of the Buddhist path is not to bring in something that we do not have but want (called "nirvāṇa" or "buddhahood") and to get rid of something that we have but do not want (called "saṃsāra" or "suffering"). The point is to realize that we already have what we think we lack and want to have (naturally pure buddha nature with its innate qualities), while we never had what we think we have and do not want (all saṃsāric obscurations).

In brief, to see what saṃsāra actually is—an illusion or a dream—is our ticket out of it. We do not have to first kick out some bad stuff (all the problems of saṃsāra) and then additionally bring in some good stuff (all the qualities of buddhahood). Just seeing that there never was any bad stuff to begin with naturally shows us that the good stuff was there all along. That is also the good news for our path: we only have one job, not two. Seeing through our illusory obscurations is sufficient to allow our buddha nature with all its qualities to shine forth in an unimpeded manner. It is not that we first have to remove some really existent obscurations and then work hard to create or cultivate all buddha qualities.

Khenpo Rinpoche explains the fourth line in Milarepa's verse on the fruition in his *Three Nails* as follows:

This mind resembles a wish-fulfilling jewel
Unborn and inconceivable, it is the dharmakāya
and its dimension of appearance is the foundation
for the form kāyas to appear in an unimpeded way
This nail is that mind's true nature is buddhahood

Buddhahood being nothing but mind's true nature refers to *our* mind's nature, not that of someone else's mind, or mind's nature in an abstract or generic sense. Often, we are in awe of the term "the nature of *the* mind," which seems like this wonderful thing, like the promised land. But how do we feel when we think about "the nature of *my* mind"? We may wonder, "What could be so great about my little confused and emotion-ridden monkey-mind? Is the nature of *my* mind really as good as the nature of *the* mind? No way it is as excellent as Buddha Śākyamuni's mind or the nature of Milarepa's mind!" Maybe when we feel good and happy, we are more optimistic about the nature of our own mind, but do we really think that the nature of our own angry or depressed mind is buddhahood? However, the dharmakāya is the true nature of every state of mind we could possibly experience. Since it is the nature of our own mind, it is nobody's but ours to discover, experience, realize, and enjoy. It has been patiently waiting for us since beginningless time and constantly tries to give us wake-up calls, but we usually ignore them. Though our mind's true being is nothing we can pinpoint, upon being realized, it fulfills all wishes we may possibly have. Therefore, it is said to be like a wish-fulfilling jewel.

This is also expressed by the famous mahāsiddha Saraha in his most well-known song, called the *People Dohā*:

> Mind as such alone is the seed of everything:
> saṃsāric existence and nirvāṇa spring from it
> To the mind that is like a wish-fulfilling jewel
> bestowing the desired results, I pay homage
> By mind being bound, you will be bound
> If it becomes free, you are free, no doubt
> By whatever it may be that fools are bound,
> through that, the wise become free swiftly

In technical terms, the utterly formless nature of the mind, just as it is, is called "dharmakāya," while "the form kāyas" manifest from it as all kinds of appearances. The form kāyas represent the dharmakāya's outreach department for others, so to speak. They perform the dharmakāya's enlightened activity for all sentient beings. The form kāyas are more or less subtle appearances with all kinds of shapes and colors which manifest for the sake of offering different beings a chance to come into indirect contact with the dharmakāya. Since the dharmakāya or mind's true unobscured nature is completely free of dualistic appearances and forms, it cannot communicate directly with ordinary beings, who are bound to exist within the framework of dualistic appearances in certain forms and can only perceive via certain forms. Therefore, the buddha mind needs some kind of go-between between it and us, which consists of the form kāyas.

From their own perspective, the dharmakāya of buddhas does not need any such form kāyas. The awakened mind of a buddha does not have to appear as Buddha Śākyamuni, Tārā, or anything at all. The nature of the mind neither has any form nor needs any form. But in order to appear to other beings who do not realize that and can only perceive and cling to something with form, buddhas, in their sambhogakāya and nirmāṇakāya manifestations, seem to have forms. Thus, the form kāyas are the altruistic educational display of the dharmakāya or the buddha mind in order to benefit all sentient beings in infinite ways, be it through teaching them the dharma or in any other ways that are needed.

In sum, Milarepa's song *Ultimate View, Meditation, Conduct, and Fruition* discusses the pith instructions of the Buddhist teachings on these four topics. It provides all the essential points in terms of the experience and realization of mahāmudrā in a succinct and profound manner. In this way, it serves as a continuous guide for mahāmudrā practitioners, as well as others, throughout their spiritual journey.

May the goodness that arises from reading, discussing, meditating on, and singing this and other songs of realization be a cause for all sentient beings to discover their innate buddha nature and to help others discover the same, so that all of us are able to live together in perfect harmony and peace.

Appendix: Milarepa's Ultimate View, Meditation, Conduct, and Fruition

The view is the wisdom of being empty
Meditation is luminosity without fixation
Conduct is a continual flow free of attachment
The fruition is nakedness bare of any stain

With the view, which is this wisdom of being empty,
there is the danger of it getting lost in mere platitudes
If certainty about the heart of the matter does not arise,
the clinging to a self will not become free through words
Therefore, the keenest certainty is absolutely essential

With meditation, this luminosity without grasping,
there is the danger of getting lost in nothing but resting
If this wisdom is not dawning from within,
even if resting is stable, it lacks the dimension of freedom
Wisdom does not arise within dullness or agitation
Therefore, undistracted mindfulness is absolutely essential

With the conduct, a continual flow free of attachment,
there is the danger of getting lost in nothing but foolish jokes
If the view and meditation do not show up as its companions,
the conduct of yogic discipline and the eight dharmas become
    friends
Therefore, to be free of clinging and obscurations is absolutely
    essential

With the fruition, this nakedness that is bare of any stain,
there is the danger of being dressed up in characteristics'
    costumes
If this delusion does not fall apart from within,
you may meditate with wishful thinking but have little idea
    about the real point
Therefore, it is absolutely essential for delusion to fall apart

Notes

1. For the entire context of this song, see Stagg 2016, 465–79.
2. All translations of Milarepa's songs in this book are mine from the Tibetan in Rus pa'i rgyan can 1981 (*Ultimate View, Meditation, Conduct, and Fruition*: 611–12).
3. The Sanskrit equivalent, *bhāvanā*, means imagining, forming in the mind, occupying one's imagination with, or directing one's thoughts to something. In this sense, the word can also refer to reflection, meditation, or contemplation. The term *bhāvanā* can also mean the application of perfumes and the like, or saturating or steeping any powder with fluid. Thus, "cultivation" or "familiarization" in this sense may be seen as "perfuming" the mindstream with virtuous imprints and liberating insights, just as a cloth might be so impregnated with a scent as to actually become inseparable from it.
4. Though the five progressive stages of meditation on emptiness presented here are labeled with the names of certain Buddhist schools, the point when practicing these meditations is not to ascertain these schools' precise positions in detail or to look for exact correspondences between these stages and the views of the actual schools whose names they bear. These stages are meant as pedagogical tools to instruct practitioners on the progression of personal insight for someone who meditates on emptiness.
5. Credits for this heading go to a button with this sentence printed on it that was given to me by Melva Forsberg many years ago; she said she is not sure anymore whether she or someone else came up with it at the time.
6. Rus pa'i rgyan can 1981, 391 (compare Stagg 2016, 237).
7. Rus pa'i rgyan can 1981, 222 (compare Stagg 2016, 34).
8. Rus pa'i rgyan can 1981, 259 (compare Stagg 2016, 78).
9. Tib. *sems nyid*.
10. Tib. *sems*.
11. Rus pa'i rgyan can 1981, 265 (compare Stagg 2016, 88).
12. Rus pa'i rgyan can 1981, 541 (compare Stagg 2016, 404).
13. Rus pa'i rgyan can 1981, 149.
14. Rus pa'i rgyan can 1981, 391 (compare Stagg 2016, 237).
15. Rus pa'i rgyan can 1981, 249 (compare Stagg 2016, 66).
16. Rus pa'i rgyan can 1981, 222 (compare Stagg 2016, 34).
17. Tib. *sgom pa sgom min goms pa yin*; *sgom pa* ("to familiarize," "to cultivate"). This is the transitive form of the intransitive verb *goms pa* ("to be or to become familiar").

18. Rus pa'i rgyan can 1981, 259 (compare Stagg 2016, 78).

19. Tib. *sems*.

20. Tib. *blo 'das*. Unfortunately, the Tibetan term *blo* is still pervasively translated as "intellect" in Buddhist writings, and *blo 'das* thus usually as "beyond the intellect" or "transcending the intellect." Besides the fact that this rendering captures only a minor part of what the Tibetan and its Sanskrit equivalent *buddhi* encompass, in Mahāmudrā and Dzogchen in particular, it is not just a question of going beyond the "intellect" (defined by the Oxford Dictionary as "the faculty of reasoning and understanding objectively, especially with regard to abstract matters," such as "having a keen intellect"). What this expression means in Mahāmudrā and Dzogchen is that what needs to be transcended is the dualistic mind in the entirety of its manifestations, which consist of all sense perceptions, emotions, thoughts, afflictions, and ego-clinging, all the way down to the most subtle, latent seeds of the ālaya-consciousness (the most fundamental level of the saṃsāric mind from which all other consciousnesses arise and where their habitual tendencies are stored). Obviously, what is understood by "intellect" makes up just a small percentage of all this and thus is a much too narrow term to be used here.

21. Rus pa'i rgyan can 1981, 724 (compare Stagg 2016, 599).

22. Khro ru klu sgrub rgya mtsho, ed. 2009, *Nges don phyag chen rgya gzhung dang bod gzhung*, 4:118–20, Chengdu, China: Si khron mi rigs dpe skrun khang.

23. Rus pa'i rgyan can 1981, 664–65 (compare Stagg 2016, 530–31).

24. Rus pa'i rgyan can 1981, 240–42 (compare Stagg 2016, 56–58).

25. Rus pa'i rgyan can 1981, 259 (compare Stagg 2016, 78–79).

26. Rus pa'i rgyan can 1981, 259 (compare Stagg 2016, 78).

Bibliography

Khenpo Tsultrim Gyamtso, Rinpoche. 2016. Translated by Shenphen Hookham. *Progressive Stages of Meditation on Emptiness*. Third edition. Criccieth, UK: Shrimala Publishing.

Rus pa'i rgyan can. 1981. *Rnal 'byor gyi dbang phyug chen po mi la ras pa'i rnam mgur*. Siling, China: Mtsho sngon mi rigs dpe skrun khang.

Stagg, Christopher, trans. 2016. *The Hundred Thousand Songs of Milarepa*. Boulder, CO: Shambhala Publications.

About the Author

Karl Brunnhölzl, MD, PhD, was originally trained as a physician. He received his systematic training in Tibetan language and Buddhist philosophy and practice at the Marpa Institute for Translators, founded by Khenpo Tsultrim Gyamtso Rinpoche, as well as the Nitartha Institute, founded by Dzogchen Ponlop Rinpoche. Since 1989 he has been a translator and interpreter from Tibetan and English. Karl Brunnhölzl is a senior teacher and translator in the Nalandabodhi community of Dzogchen Ponlop Rinpoche, as well as at the Nitartha Institute. He lives in Munich and is the author and translator of numerous texts, including *A Lullaby to Awaken the Heart: The Aspiration Prayer of Samantabhadra and Its Tibetan Commentaries* and *Luminous Melodies: Essential Dohās of Indian Mahāmudrā.*

What to Read Next from Wisdom Publications

Luminous Melodies
Karl Brunnhölzl

"These beautiful songs of experience offer glimpses into the awakened minds of the Mahāmudrā masters of India. Karl Brunnhölzl's masterful translations are a joy to read for how they express what is so often inexpressible." —His Eminence the Twelfth Zurmang Gharwang Rinpoche

Lullaby to Awaken the Heart
The Aspiration Prayer of Samantabhadra and Its Tibetan Commentaries
Karl Brunnhölzl

This monumental text outlines the profound view of Dzogchen in a nutshell and, at the same time, provides clear instructions on how to discover the wisdom of a buddha in the very midst of afflictions.

Sounds of Innate Freedom
The Indian Texts of Mahāmudrā, Volume 5
Karl Brunnhölzl

"With these vivid renditions of the songs of the Indian mahasiddhas, Karl Brunnhölzl brilliantly launches what is certain to be one of the great Buddhist scholarly projects of our time: a complete six-volume English translation of the Indian works foundational to the theory and practice of mahamudra, the great sealing of the nature of mind, which is one of the most significant and widespread of all Tibetan meditation systems." —Roger R. Jackson, author of *Mind Seeing Mind: Mahamudra and the Geluk Tradition of Tibetan Buddhism*

Drinking the Mountain Stream
Songs of Tibet's Beloved Saint, Milarepa
By Milarepa
Translated by Lama Kunga Rinpoche and Brian Cutillo

"Offers the English-speaking reader a satisfying taste of Tibetan flavored Dharma." —*Tibetan Review*

Mahamudra
A Practical Guide
His Eminence Zurmang Gharwang Rinpoche

"Gharwang Rinpoche's work serves as a definitive manual, guiding aspiring mahāmudrā students along the complete path, beginning with a clear presentation of the preliminaries, through a detailed presentation of śamatha and vipaśyanā, and concluding with enlightening instructions on the actualization of the result." —from the foreword by His Holiness the Sakya Trichen

About Wisdom Publications

Wisdom Publications is the leading publisher of classic and contemporary Buddhist books and practical works on mindfulness. To learn more about us or to explore our other books, please visit our website at wisdomexperience.org or contact us at the address below.

Wisdom Publications
199 Elm Street
Somerville, MA 02144 USA

We are a 501(c)(3) organization, and donations in support of our mission are tax deductible.

Wisdom Publications is affiliated with the Foundation for the Preservation of the Mahayana Tradition (FPMT).